The Launch Code

Master Founder-Led Sales and Boost Your Startup's Revenue Growth

Zoltan A. Vardy

Book cover and graphics by László Pintér

ISBN 979-8-9922575-0-2 (paperback)
ISBN 979-8-9922575-1-9 (ebook)

1st edition 2025
Visit the author's website at www.zoltanvardy.com for more information about related products and services.

For

Lili, *my co-founder in love and life, and*

Szofi, *the most rewarding venture of our lives.*

Contents

Why Sales Matters

"Nothing happens until someone sells something."
– Peter Drucker

As a swarm of forty 100cm-wide drones moved across the wintry skyline of central London, I stood at the edge of Buckingham Palace Gardens next to Prince Andrew, both of us captivated by the light show above. The Duke of York was clearly impressed by the drones as they moved in coordinated, holiday-themed formations, all set to music.

The thousand or so guests were equally entranced, marveling at images of a massive Christmas tree, falling snowflakes, angel silhouette, and the highlight—a 3D reindeer swiveling in the night sky. As the eight-minute drone show reached its peak, I glanced back at the crowd and was sure I glimpsed Queen Elizabeth II herself, watching from a palace window, as intrigued as the other guests.

The show was made possible by Pitch@Palace, an entrepreneurship program Prince Andrew had created to help founders accelerate their business ideas by connecting them with supporters. A startup I was advising—I'll call them Drone Show Tech—participated in the competition and earned the opportunity to deliver this spectacular drone show at the Royal Family's annual Christmas party at Buckingham Palace. It was a potential business-defining moment.

Despite numerous challenges, the founders successfully prepared the drone show in under four weeks, overcoming logistical hurdles and securing permission to fly drones over central

> *"The reason for the company's stagnation? The founders failed to understand why sales matters."*

London. This turned out to be a major coup. London's airspace is controlled by the government and subject to a strict six-week-long permit process. The founders discovered that the airspace above Buckingham Palace was an exception as it fell under the authority of the Queen. With some well-placed calls and emails, they managed to convince Prince Andrew to get his mum's approval for the drone show.

Afterward, we heard that Queen Elizabeth described the show as "quite impressive," which I like to think was her understated way of saying it was "freaking awesome."

The potential to build a buzz from such an event was enormous, yet, several years on, the company remains no larger or more commercially successful than it was in 2018. Their once best-in-class technology has been outpaced by competitors.

The reason for the company's stagnation? The founders failed to understand why sales matters.

The Road to Stagnation

To explain how we got here, let's rewind.

I met the Drone Show Tech team through one of its four co-founders who I'd supported briefly in another venture. The co-founders running the business day-to-day were technologists with advanced degrees in physics and engineering. They had studied the flight patterns of bird flocks and used this research to program drone swarms for autonomous flight. With these insights, they began creating outdoor drone light shows and had some success selling these performances to smaller festivals. I was intrigued by the business's potential in the entertainment industry and took an active role in supporting its growth.

I encouraged the founders to apply to a startup mentoring program run by Design Terminal, a Budapest-based innovation agency with which I had built a close relationship. Once they were accepted, I guided Drone Show Tech through the three-month program as their key mentor.

It didn't take long for me to realize our views on what it took to build a successful business differed greatly. I explained that commercial success lay in positioning and marketing their service, not just in perfecting the product. Yet the founders resisted even small moves in this direction, such as posting visually inspiring content online to introduce their drone shows to a broader audience.

The team's co-founder and CEO was a bit more open-minded than the others, but sales and marketing were clearly outside his comfort zone. Another co-founder responsible for developing the drone hardware feared competitors would steal their technology if they showed the drones on the internet. Plus, he likened social media promotion to what he considered "trash" posted by the likes of Kim Kardashian. Try as I might, I couldn't convince him there was a huge difference between a "wow"-inducing showreel and a celebrity's puckered-lip selfie.

I recommended the company hire a sales and marketing executive who could make up for their skills deficit and introduced them to a former sales colleague of mine. Although they began working with her, their lack of commercial focus and support made it more difficult for her to make significant progress selling drone shows to new customers.

At the time I was new to working with tech founders and didn't understand their mindset. It was completely alien to me and the source of great frustration. Today, I'd probably approach a similar situation with a bit more empathy, though I'm not sure the outcome would be much different.

Sadly, Drone Show Tech's founders never embraced their role in driving sales and marketing. They failed to capitalize on the immense publicity potential of their Buckingham Palace event, leading to stagnation while their competitors thrived. They later experimented with selling drone show management software and industrial drone services, but neither has gained meaningful commercial traction.

I wrote this book to help you avoid their fate.

If You Build It, They Will *Not* Come

Peter Drucker, a pioneer of modern management, famously said: "Nothing happens until someone sells something." He meant that the transaction between a buyer and seller powers a business and without it, a company cannot grow.

Unfortunately, many tech entrepreneurs ignore this critical principle. They are confident in the power of their product and believe their passion is enough to make it commercially successful. They don't find sales important and consider engaging with customers a nuisance. They avoid activities like marketing, contacting clients, and negotiating deals and partnerships, preferring to spend years perfecting their technology instead of testing it in the market. This behavior may support a hobby, but it certainly does not help them build a successful business.

> *"Customers will probably not discover your solution on their own, and ignoring this reality will be your downfall."*

It reminds me of the movie *Field of Dreams*. Kevin Costner plays a farmer who hears a voice whispering, "If you build it, they will come," and constructs a baseball stadium in his cornfield. Months later, a team of baseball greats magically shows up to play.

If only building a business was that easy. Customers will probably not discover your solution on their own, and ignoring this reality will be your downfall.

The harsh truth is that even the world's greatest product has no future if you don't invest time and effort into marketing it. Tech giants like Amazon, Apple, Google, Facebook, and Microsoft became so dominant not only because they created great products, but also devoted tremendous resources to explaining the value of their technology to consumers and either selling their products directly or monetizing them through other business relationships.

Professional service providers—specialists in marketing, organizational development, or finance—may not be as technology-focused, but they face similar challenges. Many built their subject matter expertise as employees and never had to create and run a business. As entrepreneurs, they must step out of their comfort zone to sell and market their services without the benefit of a reputable company brand on their business cards. They need to learn how to communicate the value of their offering and engage effectively with clients. This is their only path to commercial success.

Why Founders Avoid Selling

Some entrepreneurs understand sales is important but are reluctant to engage in the process. They feel uneasy about persuading others to buy their product or service, as if it was an imposition. Others simply hate the idea of rejection and want to avoid it at all costs.

At its most extreme, a founder's resistance stems from a conviction that if people don't see the value of their product, they don't want to spend their time explaining it. They don't understand why the world does not recognize their brilliance. While I hope you haven't reached this level of disillusionment, you might relate to the frustration of having something valuable to share but struggling to demonstrate its worth to potential clients.

Other founders recognize that sales is critical, but lack the skills and experience to execute properly. They resort to one of two approaches. The first is the "I know a guy" strategy. They can think of a few contacts who might buy their product and see this as a good foundation for their business. While this can lead to some initial clients, it has several drawbacks.

First, it is not scalable. Even if you have a broad network, it will eventually run out. Second, those you know may not be your ideal customers, which can mislead you and hinder growth. Finally, network-based selling can create a false sense of security. People who know you will give you the benefit of the doubt and raise fewer objections, while strangers will be more skeptical, requiring more convincing.

The other tactic founders employ is the "spray and pray" approach. They send thousands of cold emails or make hundreds of cold calls, hoping a few prospects will convert into sales. This strategy is often inefficient, especially for high-ticket products or services sold to enterprises. It reinforces the belief that sales and marketing are annoying—few people like getting a cold email or call. The results are unpredictable, and rarely offer a good return on investment, making it a poor foundation for scaling a business.

Ask yourself honestly: "Which of these categories do I fall into?"

1. I don't think sales and marketing is important.

2. I know sales matters but must overcome my resistance.

3. I recognize that sales is critical but lack the skills and experience to sell effectively.

No matter what your answer, know this: there is no shortcut. Until you tackle sales and marketing head-on, you won't build a sustainable business. This means people won't use your product, you won't receive the financial rewards, and—most importantly—your vision for building a breakthrough business will go unrealized.

You Can Learn to Sell

The good news is that sales and marketing skills can be learned. No matter how impossible it may seem, you can master founder-led sales.

You can also lose that discomfort that often makes selling feel bothersome or insincere.

This book gives you a blueprint to get you started. It explains the *mindset* you need to adopt, the *strategies* you need to learn, and the *tactics* to apply in order to sell more effectively with less effort. It guides you step by step through a structured approach that will help you accelerate your revenue growth and scale your business.

Many founders who once felt lost have shared that applying this approach was like turning the lights on in a dark room. "I now understand how sales and marketing work together," David Pataki of Enrol Consulting told me. "I know the processes I need to introduce, the KPIs I need to set and track, what resources I need to get the job done, and what goals I should set for myself. *The Launch Code* gave my company a complete structure, strategy, and focus."

As you gain momentum, you'll no longer shy away from sales. You may even find that you start enjoying it. I've worked with numerous founders who now take pride in their sales efforts,

> *"No matter how impossible it may seem, you can master founder-led sales."*

no longer fearing rejection and discouragement. Most importantly, they've realized that effective selling is crucial to building the long-term, sustainable business they've always dreamed of creating.

In sales, as in anything, you need to walk before you can run. Although artificial intelligence tools and platforms have gained significant attention in recent years, they cannot replace the core principles of sales and marketing. They can enhance efficiency but are useless if you deliver an unclear message to the wrong target market using an ineffective sales channel.

This book is designed for founders who are skilled at creating products or services and are comfortable with technology but need guidance on sales and marketing. It's equally relevant for professional experts who need guidance in how to sell their services. There's no confusing jargon or complex technical solutions here—just the fundamentals of effective sales and marketing.

What You Can Expect

This material is based on *The Launch Code*, the framework I teach founders so they can accelerate revenue growth for their businesses. The book begins by covering essential mindset principles, then moves into actionable strategies structured around the three core pillars. It concludes with a practical section on tactics to handle specific situations you'll encounter as you apply these lessons to your business.

Chapter 1, "**The Pain of Sales,**" explains why selling is difficult at first, and why you, the founder, must do it yourself in the early stages of your business. Embracing this challenge is vital for your growth. Eventually, selling becomes easier as confusion and anxiety dissipate, and you experience wins that boost your confidence and know-how.

Chapter 2, "**The Problem-Solution Connection,**" shifts your focus from pushing products to solving customer problems, making the process more customer-centric. It explains why you must focus on solving a specific problem and define a customer niche to become a "must-have" product or service.

Chapter 3 introduces *The Launch Code*'s first pillar, "**Focus Your Offer and Message.**" To win clients, you must clearly define the problem you solve, identify who benefits, and demonstrate why your target customer should choose you. This chapter shows you how to bring your value proposition to life through a well-crafted product offering and effective client messaging communicated through various sales tools and marketing platforms.

Chapter 4 introduces the second pillar of *The Launch Code*: **"Structure Your Client Acquisition."** Knowing *whom* to approach, and *how* to approach them is key to closing deals with minimal effort. In this chapter, you'll learn how to implement and test the three main forms of client acquisition: outbound sales, partnerships, and inbound marketing.

With a strong offer and client acquisition strategy in place, Chapter 5 tackles *The Launch Code's* third pillar: **"Scale Your Operations."** You'll learn how to set goals and track your performance so you can assess and refine your sales activities.

"This material is based on The Launch Code, the framework I teach founders so they can accelerate revenue growth for their businesses."

Finally, you'll understand how to develop an empowered team that covers all key sales and marketing functions, allowing you to focus on growth and create a scalable organization.

Chapter 6, **"Navigating Real-World Scenarios,"** provides practical advice on managing the speed bumps you'll encounter as you apply these sales and marketing strategies to your business. This chapter prepares you to navigate the most common obstacles as well as manage special situations, like selling to large corporations or expanding into new countries.

Chapter 7, **"Putting *The Launch Code* to Work,"** introduces two practical exercises to help you implement *The Launch Code* in your business. The *Destination Plan* guides you in envisioning where you want to take your business, while the *Blast Off! Blueprint* helps you focus on the actions needed to reach your destination. I emphasize the importance of taking immediate action, so you can experience the transformative impact this approach will have on your revenue growth.

Why Listen to Me?

You might wonder how I'm qualified to teach you how to sell.

I was born in Pittsburgh, Pennsylvania, to a Hungarian American family with no business background. My parents were professors, and did not hold sales in high regard: *"I know you can learn how to sell because I did too."* when salespeople called our house, my mother pretended to be the maid, and informed the person calling that the Vardy family had moved to Europe, so they'd never call back.

I grew up a shy, reserved kid with an ethnic name—certainly not part of the popular crowd. While I was a good student with a strong family background, I doubt my friends or family ever imagined I'd become an international businessman, closing $2 billion in sales over a thirty-year career.

I know this isn't the typical "rags-to-riches" story, but I share it anyway for one reason: I know you can learn how to sell because I did too. The sales and marketing principles in this book aren't based on innate talent or magic—they're practical insights and skills I developed as an adult through dedicated learning, mentorship, and hands-on experience.

From Beginner to Entrepreneur

After graduating from Cornell University with a degree in European history, I initially planned to become a journalist.

At age twenty-two, I launched a business weekly in Hungary on behalf of the Swiss publishing company Ringier, filling a gap in the post-Communist publishing market. This gave me my first taste of building a business from scratch, adapting a product concept, hiring a team, and shaping marketing strategy.

I cemented my transition from journalism to sales and business development via stints at *USA Today International* and Cartoon Network in London, and at CBS's corporate sales and marketing division in Los Angeles. After spending a few years immersed in California's late-nineties dotcom boom, surrounded by ambitious founders launching internet startups, I caught the entrepreneurial bug.

My brother and I launched a network of local-language web portals in Eastern Europe, based in Budapest. Our goal was to sell the business to an American dotcom that wanted a foothold in the region, but the 2000 dotcom crash stymied our plans. We eventually sold the company to local investors. It wasn't the life-changing exit we'd hoped for, but it was a solid outcome given the circumstances.

Becoming a Sales Leader

I returned to the corporate world as commercial director at TV2, one of Hungary's two national TV networks. I won the job by sending a cold email to the CEO of its parent company, SBS Broadcasting, with the subject line: "Boost your revenues with one key hire."

This outreach led to a successful eight-year tenure, during which my team and I grew the broadcaster's annual revenue from €60 million to

€100 million in three years. We achieved this remarkable growth by focusing on ideal customers, refining our message, engaging proactively, setting goals, and tracking performance—all principles that would later form the foundation of *The Launch Code*.

I was eventually promoted to vice president of sales for TV2's parent company managing ad revenue across twenty-six channels in eight European markets. Following SBS Broadcasting's sale to Germany's ProSiebenSat1 Media, I became CEO of TV2 and later regional CEO of five TV channels in the group.

I left this job in late 2010, and spent a few years teaching, investing, and working on ventures before rejoining the corporate world in 2014 as senior vice president of ad sales for NBCUniversal's international entertainment networks. Though overseeing $150 million in ad revenue for fifty-five channels in thirty countries was rewarding, I eventually felt too far removed from the frontline of sales and moved on after three years.

Dedicated to Helping Founders

After leaving NBCUniversal, I became deeply engaged in Europe's startup scene. I mentored dozens of early-stage businesses and invested in successful ones like Brainient, Dexory, and Antavo, where I eventually became chairman.

This experience brought to light the sales and marketing challenges many founders encounter, inspiring me to develop *The Launch Code*. Drawing on strategies I had honed throughout my career—techniques that felt instinctive to me but were game-changing for the entrepreneurs I mentored—I created a framework to help founders effectively sell and market to business customers. Since its inception,

The Launch Code has fueled revenue growth for over 200 startups across twenty-six countries, delivered through workshops, mentoring, and a video course.

This latest chapter of my career has been one of the most rewarding, as I've witnessed firsthand how the mindset, strategies, and tactics shared in this book have helped founders build the businesses they've dreamed about.

I look forward to helping you achieve the same success.

Who Should Read This Book?

I wrote this book for entrepreneurs, not hustlers.

If you expect overnight success, believe in "get-rich-quick" schemes, or don't care about the product or service you offer, read no further.

This guide is for founders who are committed to solving a problem that matters to them. They're willing to put in the work to build a sustainable company, yet they struggle with making sales and marketing work for their business.

"I wrote this book for entrepreneurs, not hustlers."

Perhaps you're like the entrepreneur I met who spent years developing an app to evaluate the health of trees in city centers. His goal was to save thousands of trees from needless destruction. I thought it was a wild idea, but for him, it was a passion. He understood, though, that he could only transform that passion into a viable business if he learned how to sell and market his product to paying customers— which is exactly what he did.

If your high-ticket product or service tackles a meaningful problem for business customers, I'll teach you how to sell and market it. What matters most is your willingness to show up, focus, and commit to changing your mindset, applying certain strategies and tactics, and ultimately, learning how to sell.

If that sounds like you, let's dive in and get to work!

PART 1

MINDSET

Henry Ford famously said, "Whether you think you can, or think you can't, you're right," underscoring the profound role mindset plays in determining your success. Nowhere is this more evident than in sales.

If you view closing deals as an overwhelming and insurmountable task, it will be. But if you embrace sales as an opportunity to learn and grow, that mindset will set you on the path to long-term success. For founders, how you think about sales can make or break your business.

Building the right mindset begins with embracing what I call the "pain of sales." As a technically focused founder, stepping into the sales role may seem intimidating, but it's a necessary challenge. Without a dedicated sales team, the responsibility falls on your shoulders. While it's tempting to delay or avoid it, the most successful founders know that confronting this discomfort head-on is not just important—it's a powerful step toward taking control of your company's future.

Underpinning the proper mindset is understanding that sales isn't about pushing products—it's about solving problems. The goal is to understand your client's challenges and show how your solution addresses them. By creating a strong problem-solution connection, you turn sales from a manipulative process into a collaborative conversation. This approach helps you build trust, foster meaningful relationships, and position yourself as a partner, not just a vendor.

Finally, a sales mindset is built on persistence. Every founder faces rejection, setbacks, and failures, especially when engaging with potential customers. The right mindset allows you to learn from these experiences, refine your approach, and remain confident that the right opportunities will align with your solution. With persistence and a willingness to adapt, you'll transform sales into a driving force for your business's success.

CHAPTER 1

The Pain of Sales

"You gotta have stuff that sucks to have stuff that's cool."
– Beavis and Butthead

Podim is a vibrant tech and startup conference held annually in Maribor, Slovenia, the second city of a small European country adjacent to the Adriatic Sea. I attended virtually in 2021 due to the COVID-19 pandemic, but in 2023, I was pleased to participate in person.

The Maribox building, where the conference took place, was a short stroll from my hotel. The venue is normally a popular entertainment spot thanks to its multiplex cinemas, arcade games, and bars. This day, however, it was packed with over 1,500 entrepreneurs, investors, and technology experts from Southcentral Europe.

As I moved through the bustling crowd, I ran into the event organizer, Urban Lapajne, who seemed calm and confident about the conference's likely success. On the escalator to the first-floor theaters,

I chatted with my friend Julien Coustaury, the tall, energetic co-founder of Fil Rouge Capital, the region's most active venture capital investor. We were all gearing up for two days of presentations, panels, and networking, hoping for glimpses of tech advancements shaping our lives—like the previous year when American engineering and robotics company Boston Dynamics sent a robot dog to interact with conference attendees.

I had three objectives: deliver a keynote, host a sales workshop, and build relationships with potential clients and partners. My speech, titled "Gods vs. Frauds", explored the differences between legendary tech entrepreneurs and those later exposed as charlatans. Think Steve Jobs versus Elizabeth Holmes. The feedback I'd gotten after my talk lifted my spirits and set the tone for my sales workshop the next morning.

"You Literally Saved My Business."

As the evening set in, I joined other attendees for dinner and drinks in the rear of the venue that featured a terrace and bar overlooking the Drava River. I was pleasantly surprised to run into my client Simon Neal for the first time since we'd worked together the previous spring.

Simon, a British entrepreneur living in Croatia, founded CampMap, a software-as-a-service (SaaS) tool that helps campsites share details of their facilities with guests. He's an intelligent and driven founder, passionate about creating a product that amplifies his love for camping. Like many tech founders, he believed in his product but struggled to sell it to paying customers. To tackle this challenge, Simon signed up for *The Launch Code* personal mentoring program.

Curious about his progress since completing the program, I asked Simon for his feedback. His response was simple but impactful.

"Zoltan," he told me. "You literally saved my business."

I was surprised, flattered, and proud to hear how much my framework had helped Simon accelerate CampMap's revenue growth. As we chatted on the terrace, beers in hand, Simon shared how *The Launch Code* had changed his perspective on sales, and how he'd implemented its strategies and techniques.

In September 2022, CampMap faced a critical crossroads. After early success in Croatia, the company had secured funding to expand into Germany but struggled to close new deals. With only three months of operating funds left, Simon dove into *The Launch Code*, rallying his team and transforming as many employees as possible into salespeople. The alternative—slashing staff to a bare minimum— might have kept the business afloat, but would have derailed its growth potential.

"Zoltan," he told me. "You literally saved my business."

What followed was a nerve-wracking race against time: learning how to sell before the money ran out. Simon encountered the pain of sales firsthand—the frustration of navigating rejection, self-doubt, and intense pressure, all magnified by the trial and error of mastering an unfamiliar skill. It was gut-wrenching but unavoidable.

"We put your structured process into action: this is how you reach out to people with emails, that's how you generate the content. When you talk to clients, this is how you present your product," Simon told me. "We completely changed our product offering to include an onboarding fee and three options, and we also updated our website messaging."

Gradually, these changes paid off. CampMap began winning new clients and gained the breathing room it so desperately needed.

Today, CampMap's recurring revenue has doubled year-on-year. The team now closes deals with at least 50 percent of prospects, adding forty new clients in 2023 alone. They've expanded from three markets to eleven, including the United States, and are exploring opportunities in Australia and New Zealand to counterbalance Europe's seasonal downturns during winter.

Still, Simon acknowledges there's room to grow. "We're not perfect at sales," he admits, "but we're way, way better than we were."

Sales Hurts, but Not Forever

In the words of iconic 1990's MTV characters Beavis and Butthead: "You gotta have stuff that sucks to have stuff that's cool." The lesson is simple: while no one seeks out pain, it's often a necessary step toward achieving meaningful goals.

> *"While no one seeks out pain, it's often a necessary step toward meaningful goals."*

For tech founders, selling can be one of those painful steps. It pushes you beyond your comfort zone, challenging you to embrace a skill that may not come naturally. Whether you're aiming to build the next unicorn—a company valued at $1 billion or more—create a steadily growing startup, or operate a comfortable lifestyle business, mastering sales is essential to generate predictable revenue and scale.

At its core, sales is about identifying a prospect's problem and clearly communicating how your solution solves it, motivating them to buy. This connection can only be truly understood through direct involvement in the sales process—a practice known as founder-led sales.

Founder-led sales offers two transformative benefits:

Customer Connection and Feedback: Engaging directly with your target clients helps you deeply understand their needs, providing invaluable feedback to refine both your pitch and your product. Without this connection, you risk misunderstanding your ideal customers or missing the mark on the problems your solution addresses.

Foundation for Delegation: Founder-led sales equips you to hire and train others effectively. When the time comes to delegate, you'll have the insights needed to select the right person to lead sales and marketing, and you'll be able to evaluate their performance confidently.

You might argue that you'd rather focus on building technology and delegate sales to a professional. While delegation is an option for later, in the early stages, it's not going to work. As the founder, you know your product best and are its most passionate advocate. Like it or not, you are your company's chief sales officer.

In rare cases, you may have a co-founder with complementary sales and marketing skills. Even so, as a product-focused founder, you must understand your market and customer needs to ensure your technology aligns with them.

The good news? The pain of sales doesn't last forever. If you persist and embrace the discomfort, you'll eventually achieve product-market fit—what Silicon Valley investor Marc Andreessen describes as "being in a good market with a product that can satisfy that market." Once you reach that milestone, the hardest part will be behind you.

The rest of this chapter will guide you step-by-step to bridge the gap between where you are now and that happy place.

Getting Sales Right is a Process

Patience is essential. Developing the perfect sales and marketing strategy takes time, much like learning a

"Like it or not, you are your company's chief sales officer."

new language or mastering a musical instrument. Improving your skills and knowledge is a gradual process that requires persistence.

Selling is painful because it's inherently iterative, with no guaranteed path to success. Some days will bring breakthroughs, while others will leave you questioning what on earth you're doing wrong. Progress and emotions fluctuate, making the process as unpredictable as it is challenging.

Initially, you'll rely on assumptions about what might work. By engaging in sales, you'll transform those assumptions into testable hypotheses, refining them until you discover what truly resonates with your business and customers.

For example, you might start by identifying the problem your product solves and realize that several types of companies share this issue. As you dig deeper, you'll notice these groups have different budgets and decision-making processes. Most likely, you'll focus on the segments with more money and faster decisions.

Next, you'll refine your messaging and presentation to compel these companies to act. You'll also assess communication channels— outbound sales, partnerships, and more—and measure key performance indicators (KPIs) to identify which methods drive the best results. This cyclical process helps align your offerings with the needs of your target audience.

Even after achieving product-market fit, growth may require expansion into new markets, restarting the iteration process. While this may reintroduce the pain of sales, each cycle will feel more familiar, less overwhelming, and far shorter.

How I Found Product-Market Fit

To illustrate how this process works, let me share my journey in creating *The Launch Code*.

Throughout my career, I've gained extensive sales and marketing experience worldwide, closing hundreds of deals with diverse customers as both a corporate executive and entrepreneur. Yet, even with this background, I still experienced the pain of sales.

> *"Selling is painful because it's inherently iterative, with no guaranteed path to success."*

When I began, I offered general business mentorship to founders, but quickly realized that their biggest challenge wasn't leadership or organizational issues—it was generating revenue. Recognizing this, I focused on a problem I was uniquely qualified to solve: sales and marketing to business customers, also known as B2B sales.

Next, I started targeting small businesses, including both tech startups and traditional companies. While both groups wanted to grow sales, I found tech founders to be a better fit. They were ambitious, aimed to build global businesses, and excelled at product development while struggling with sales and marketing. My experience scaling international businesses gave me credibility with them, which helped me build trust quickly.

Identifying my target customer took time, but I wasn't done yet.

As I marketed my services to founders, I discovered that the term "startup" was applied broadly—from people with just an idea to scale-ups with 100+ employees and significant revenue. The former focused solely on product development and lacked funding, while the latter had a sales leader in place and well-established strategy.

I needed to zero in on the sweet spot: businesses with seed funding, a foothold in their market, and some paying customers, but which were struggling to generate predictable, recurring revenue. These were my ideal clients.

Reaching this level of clarity wasn't easy. It took over three years of trial and error to refine my focus, and the process was often frustrating. But the effort paid off. Knowing exactly who I was selling to enabled me to create *The Launch Code* and build a successful business.

I won't claim the pain of sales is gone entirely—I still experience it as I evolve my offering. But now, it's a far more manageable and familiar process.

My sales journey wasn't linear, and yours won't be either. Even with decades of experience, I needed time to identify what wasn't working and adjust. There's no shortcut for figuring out what works—you learn it one step at a time.

Don't Believe the Hustler's Hype

The approach I've outlined stands in contrast with what some "hustlers" want you to believe is the best way to build a business. These social media influencers, often pictured with flashy cars and glamorous girlfriends, claim you can achieve overnight success by gaming the system. It's more likely you're the one getting gamed.

Achieving real success in sales and business is rarely that simple. While some people do get lucky, relying on good fortune alone isn't a sustainable or repeatable strategy.

Much like lottery winners who quickly lose their wealth due to poor financial management, hustlers who avoid doing the hard work often end up unfulfilled. True business success comes from the effort you put in, which makes your achievements that much more rewarding. To truly appreciate success, you need to earn it.

I aim to help you turn your product and vision into reality—not just spin a wheel. To do this, you'll need to shift your mindset. While avoiding sales may seem tempting, embracing it will make the journey worthwhile.

"There's no shortcut for figuring out what works—you learn it one step at a time."

Combining tech skills with strong sales abilities is a powerful one-two punch and will increase your chances of success. The more you embrace and develop sales skills, the more you'll not only tolerate but even enjoy the process as you see positive results.

Accept that you won't be perfect from the start. Start small and learn valuable lessons about connecting with and serving customers. Over time, you'll identify the problem you solve, who you solve it for, and the best way to reach your ideal customers. You'll improve the quality of your engagements, shorten your sales cycle, and close more deals.

Action Audit: Building a Growth Engine

Aleksander Niemczyk of Ruby Logic embraced the pain of sales and turned his business into a thriving growth engine. We met in October 2021 at Wolves Summit, a startup conference held in Poland.

Ruby Logic had spent years developing bespoke software for various clients, including ones in precision manufacturing industries like automotive and aerospace. Aleksander identified a need in this industry: clients lacked a tool to store, assign, and track tasks resulting from audits of their manufacturing processes. In response, he created Action Audit, a SaaS platform that reduces internal audit time by 70 percent with a paperless solution.

Despite launching Action Audit four years earlier, Aleksander had only six paying customers, mostly from Poland. He recognized that while an expert in software, he needed to improve his sales and marketing skills to scale. Eager to learn, he sought a sales mentor.

From Goals to Results

Aleksander and I began our collaboration by setting three goals:

- Create a clear sales message.

- Develop a repeatable, results-driven sales process.

- Align long-term goals with daily actions to maximize productivity.

As we worked through *The Launch Code*, Aleksander gained confidence and became more comfortable with sales and marketing. He started regularly posting content on LinkedIn, sharing his expertise to boost his business's visibility and credibility. By the end of the program, Aleksander could easily explain Action Audit's value proposition to prospects, improved his partnerships and inbound marketing, and attracted customers from across Europe and the United States.

In just over two years, Aleksander expanded his client base from six to fifty-two, including both small and large enterprises. SaaS subscription revenue surged by 400 percent, making Action Audit the company's primary revenue source, surpassing bespoke projects, which now represent only 20 percent of the business.

His customer base grew from Poland to six European countries, which now account for 40 percent of total revenue. The company gained significant advantage through partnerships with consultants in Germany, who recommend Action Audit to ideal customers. Aleksander is now expanding into retail and hotel chains—industries with vast growth potential.

Embracing Sales Means Business

Aleksander's willingness to embrace the pain of sales is impressive. "I heard a lot of stories about companies who tried to hire a sales specialist without founder involvement, and it didn't work at all," he says. "You have to hear questions and objections from prospects to move forward."

He credits *The Launch Code* with helping him focus on key activities. He has increased his time spent on sales and marketing from 5 percent to 60 percent. He remains the primary sales leader, supported by one sales and marketing executive.

Aleksander is now far more confident and prouder of his achievements—a stark contrast to the reserved, unsure founder I first met in Poland. "Sales was completely odd and stressful for me," he recalls. "It wasn't in my nature to convince people to buy something. I wanted them to spot the features and value by themselves. Now I feel quite comfortable in sales meetings."

Aleksander's journey demonstrates the transformative power of embracing sales for business growth.

* * *

Key Takeaways

- **Embrace Founder-Led Sales**: Though it can be uncomfortable at first, early-stage tech founders must engage in sales to understand their market and customers. This hands-on approach helps refine the pitch, improve the product, and build a sustainable business.

- **Sales is a Learning Process**: Achieving product-market fit is a gradual process. Founders must test assumptions, refine messaging, and adapt based on customer feedback, so they build the skills needed to scale and eventually delegate sales.

- **Ignore the Hustler's Myth**: Sustainable growth requires patience, effort, and skill development, not shortcuts or luck. By combining technical expertise with sales skills, founders can build strong customer relationships, streamline sales, and achieve lasting success.

CHAPTER 2

The Problem-Solution Connection

"Selling is about helping someone solve an important problem."

– Dan Lovinger

David Pataki is a soft-spoken, introspective tech founder in his mid-forties, intensely focused on solving problems for himself and his clients. Before we met, he had grown his software business, Enrol Consulting, to support a team of twenty-five engineers. But his revenue relied heavily on two corporate clients, and he struggled to expand his customer base.

Early on, David had identified a common challenge faced by large corporations: siloed data spread across incompatible databases, which made it nearly impossible to extract actionable insights. Imagine a bank with separate customer relationship management (CRM) systems, payment solutions, and social media platforms, all unable to communicate with each other. Recognizing this as a costly problem, David developed a solution—a consolidated, user-friendly dashboard that enabled managers to access and analyze their data seamlessly.

David had already identified a powerful problem-solution connection, which would become the foundation of his success. At the time, however, he struggled to convey its value to new prospects.

"You Took the 'Voodoo' Out of Sales."

When I met David, he described sales as an uncomfortable, mysterious process—what he jokingly called "black magic." He lacked a structured approach to targeting prospects and felt unqualified to engage them.

We began working on his mindset and approach, using *The Launch Code* framework. By breaking it down into learnable steps, David began to see sales not as an intimidating art form but as a logical process. He practiced communicating his solution's value, structuring his outreach, and positioning himself as an authority. He even started posting LinkedIn videos where he interviewed professionals at industry conferences—small but significant steps that demonstrated his growing confidence.

David's turning point came during a mentoring session, when he mentioned a recent deal concluded after he doubled the price of his entry-level package—from €5,000 to €10,000. Curious, I asked if he had added new features. His response was simple: "I just realized the value of what I was offering and presented it with confidence. The client immediately saw how much time and money they'd save and agreed without hesitation."

This shift in mindset, worth thousands of euros in added revenue, didn't require changes to his product—only a clearer articulation of its value. By connecting his solution directly to his client's problem and confidently communicating that alignment, David transformed how he approached sales and unlocked significant growth.

As David later told me, "You took the voodoo out of sales and marketing."

David's example demonstrates that sales isn't magic; it's about aligning solutions with genuine client needs and articulating that alignment clearly. Founders who understand and master this skill can turn their product or expertise into compelling offers that clients can't ignore—no "voodoo" required.

Selling Gets a Bad Rap

It's no surprise that so many founders take a dim view of sales and marketing. Movies and TV shows frequently depict salespeople as slick con artists—like used car salesmen eager to deceive customers into buying things they don't need. Social media doesn't help either, with young hustlers promising overnight success and untold riches through minimal effort. The way sales is portrayed creates the perception that selling is a win-lose game where the salesperson wins by tricking the buyer.

I used to feel the same way. Growing up, I thought of sales as a dubious profession, and couldn't have imagined that it would become a significant part of my career.

My initial plan was to become a journalist. I interned as a college student at Reuters and *The Wall Street Journal Europe*, and immersed myself in the world of media. I soon realized that my skills in crafting messages and managing projects were more highly valued on the business side of the industry. This led me to a marketing role at *USA*

Today International, and eventually, to Turner Broadcasting, where I worked to expand Cartoon Network across Europe.

It was in this environment that I began to see sales in a different light. Hired to manage ad sales for Central and Eastern Europe, I quickly faced the challenge of meeting revenue targets. The pressure triggered my discomfort with sales and left me feeling uneasy and unprepared.

But everything changed during a business trip to Moscow, where my boss, Dan Lovinger, and I were planning to meet with advertisers. On our way into town, we rode in a taxi along one of the Russian capital's sprawling six-lane avenues. I shared my mental struggles with Dan and asked for his advice. What he said to me completely shifted my perspective:

> *"The way sales is portrayed creates the perception that selling is a win-lose game where the salesperson wins by tricking the buyer."*

"Selling isn't about pushing something on someone who doesn't need it," he said. "It's about helping them solve an important problem. And let's face it—everyone likes getting help with their problems."

Dan's response was a lightbulb moment. That's when it clicked for me—sales isn't about selling products; it's about solving problems. This shift in perspective set me on a new career path, one dedicated to helping clients find solutions to their challenges.

The Path to €100 Million

In August 2002, I had a golden opportunity to put Dan's insight into practice. I became the Commercial Director at TV2 in Hungary, which was in crisis. The channel had lost its market-leading position to rival RTL Klub, and revenues were plummeting. Over the next three years, my team and I turned things around, growing annual revenue from €60 million to €100 million, increasing our ad market share despite declining viewership. We became the star performer in SBS Broadcasting's portfolio of twenty-six channels in eight countries.

The key to our success was leveraging the problem-solution connection.

When I started, I inherited a demotivated sales team. My American-style enthusiasm clashed with their cynicism, born from shrinking viewership and lost revenues. It was clear that I needed to shift their mindset toward a brighter future we could create together.

One evening, as I drove across Budapest's iconic Széchenyi Chain Bridge, a bold vision came to my mind: we would increase TV2's revenue from 16 billion HUF (€60 million) to 25 billion HUF (€100 million) by 2005. The slogan "25 in 2005" became a rallying cry for the team, and even though they were skeptical, I did my best to convince them it was a stretch target worth pursuing.

I reinforced this goal at every opportunity. When we had a bad month, I reminded my team that our target was "25 in 2005"; when we had a good month, I encouraged them with, "We're getting closer to '25 in 2005'". In 2003, the ad market expanded more than expected, and we began attracting new clients. The year after, our momentum continued to grow as both the market and my team embraced our new sales approach. By 2005, we were executing our plan like a well-oiled machine. A goal that once seemed impossible was now within reach.

Selling Marketing Solutions, Not Airtime

The shift came when we stopped selling airtime and started solving problems for our customers.

TV2's previous sales strategy was simple: "Here's some airtime; would you like to buy it?" As the network lost market leadership, this approach stalled, making the channel's airtime a devaluing commodity. Offering discounts became the previous management's only tool to keep customers.

I shifted our focus to understanding clients' marketing challenges and offering comprehensive packages. Our new mantra became, "We offer marketing solutions." This enabled us to build strategic relationships and create concept-driven partnerships, combining airtime, sponsorships, online advertising, branded events, and even merchandise.

We sometimes created ideas from scratch, like the summer beach concert tour we hosted for Dreher beer. In other cases, we leveraged TV2 programs, like *Big Brother* and the local version of *Pop Idol*, called *Megasztár*, which became our flagship commercial powerhouse. We used these programs to establish strategic marketing relationships with brands like Pepsi, Procter & Gamble, and LG.

This solutions-driven approach also changed how we negotiated, as we emphasized value over price. We stopped offering discounts so readily and became known as tough but fair negotiators—leaving behind TV2's previous reputation as a desperate pushover.

The impact was undeniable. By 2005, our revenue reached 24.6 billion HUF (€98.5 million)—just shy of our ambitious goal of "25 in 2005," but still a major achievement and a source of enormous pride for everyone involved.

My sales team's efforts led to my promotion to vice president of ad sales at SBS Broadcasting, then CEO of TV2, and eventually leadership of the regional TV group. When I left in 2010, my team gave me a parting gift: an image of my face styled like the iconic Barack Obama poster with the words "Yes we can."

We Solve Problems Every Day

The last time you planned a holiday, you likely did so to solve a problem: perhaps you needed a relaxing break from work or wanted to spend quality time with your family. Whatever your ultimate destination, you chose it to meet a specific need.

You may not realize this, but every decision, big or small, is about solving problems—whether it's choosing a school for your kids or selecting your route to work. Problem-solving is so ingrained in our daily lives that we barely notice it.

This perspective may help you see that sales isn't something you should fear. Both buyers and sellers are simply engaged in a natural exchange of solutions. The seller's job is to offer a good solution, and the buyer's job is to choose the one that fits their needs. The only difference between buying and selling is our position in this exchange.

As you gain experience and more people thank you for solving their problems, your confidence will grow. You may slowly come to tolerate sales. In time, you may even come to love it, knowing that what you offer is truly valuable.

A Perfect Solution to a Specific Problem

To create a powerful problem-solution connection, you must position yourself as the perfect solution to a specific problem—not a potential solution to many problems.

Consider this: When I injured my knee trail running, I didn't consult a general practitioner or a cardiologist—I sought out an orthopedist who specializes in knee injuries. He knew exactly how to diagnose and treat my condition. I didn't feel pressured or manipulated; I felt grateful and happy to pay for his expertise.

By focusing solely on his area of specialization, my orthopedist ensures he attracts the right patients, even if it narrows his potential market. His expertise makes him indispensable to those who need him most. This principle applies to any business or service: when you solve a specific problem perfectly, you create immense value and build trust.

> *"Problem-solving is so ingrained in our daily lives that we barely notice it."*

This concept breaks down into answering three core questions.

What Problem Do You Solve?

Your first task is to identify *what* specific problem you solve.

The narrower your focus, the more likely your audience will notice and remember you. Think of your focus as the tip of a spear cutting through the wall of competing messages. Trying to solve multiple problems is like wielding a blunt instrument: it lacks precision and impact.

Jeff Bezos understood this when he founded Amazon in 1995. He didn't set out to sell everything to everyone. Instead, he targeted a specific audience—young men, the most active internet users at the time—and solved a specific problem: accessing hard-to-find books. Once he had tested his business model and logistic capabilities, he expanded into music and films, eventually turning Amazon into the juggernaut it is today—an e-commerce platform selling anything from electronics to kitchenware to 320 million customers each year.

> *"As Confucius wisely said, 'The man who chases two rabbits, catches neither.'"*

Narrowing your focus may feel limiting at first, but it's easier to broaden your reach after proving your effectiveness than to pivot from being too broad.

Who Do You Solve It For?

Next, clearly define *who* is your ideal customer.

Many founders mistakenly believe targeting a broad audience increases their chances of success, but the opposite is true. Focusing on a niche allows you to connect more deeply with your audience, build trust, and establish authority.

As Confucius wisely said, "The man who chases two rabbits, catches neither." The same principle applies in sales: casting your net too widely spreads your efforts thin. Instead, focus on a specific, active part of the pond (market) where the fish (ideal customers) are most abundant. By narrowing your focus, you'll catch more fish with less effort, making your sales efforts far more effective.

Rather than limiting your potential, this approach positions you as a trusted authority within your niche, creating a loyal customer base that can grow over time.

How Do You Solve It Better Than Others?

Finally, differentiate *how* your solution stands out.

What makes your product or service unique or superior? Whether it's speed, precision, ease of use, or a proprietary methodology, your competitive advantage is what compels customers to choose you over alternatives.

Avoid defining your competition too narrowly. For instance, if you develop a writing app, your competitors aren't just other apps—they might include pen and paper or voice recording tools. Understanding the full competitive landscape ensures your solution remains distinct and compelling.

Sales is Also About Saying "No"

Once you embrace this principle, it transforms not just how you sell but also how you approach prospects. You gain the confidence to say "no" to opportunities that don't align with your solution—even when it means walking away from short-term revenue. Saying no isn't a sign of failure; it's a sign of integrity.

I've encountered this situation many times in my career. For example, I once spoke with a Swedish founder in Seattle who wanted to know if *The Launch Code* could help him grow his revenue. He had launched a $25-per-month SaaS tool for engineers, targeting solopreneurs and small businesses. While his product was impressive, it didn't align with my solution. *The Launch Code* is designed to help founders sell high-ticket solutions to mid-to-enterprise-level businesses—not to optimize low-cost SaaS sales.

Instead of trying to fit him into my framework, I told him honestly that digital advertising, which wasn't my area of expertise, was likely his best path forward. He appreciated my transparency, and while this interaction didn't result in a sale for me, it encouraged him to find a more appropriate solution.

When you view sales as solving problems, this kind of honesty becomes second nature. It shifts the focus from simply closing deals to creating value and building trust. Instead of feeling pressured to convince prospects, you start evaluating whether your solution genuinely meets their needs. Sales becomes a process you can feel proud of—not because you've closed deals, but because you've genuinely helped people along the way.

And here's the surprising part: saying no can often lead to better outcomes in the long run. Prospects respect authenticity. They remember the person who prioritized their needs over making a sale. In some cases, those same prospects return later when they find themselves in a situation better suited to your expertise—or they refer others who are.

My Problem-Solution Connection

Just as you need to identify the problem you solve, and for whom and how, I did the same when designing *The Launch Code*. Through mentoring, I recognized that tech founders often struggle with B2B sales and needed a blueprint that shows them how to sell and market their product effectively.

I identified three core challenges they face and created a solution for each.

First, they struggle to clearly communicate their product's value, leaving prospects confused about what they're selling. The solution is a straightforward value proposition, clear product options, and messaging that engages potential buyers to explore further (Pillar One).

Second, many founders lack a structured customer acquisition strategy, leading to inconsistent results from random outreach. The solution is to target ideal customers through a mix of outbound sales, partnerships, and inbound marketing, testing each channel to determine the best fit for the business (Pillar Two).

Finally, founders have difficulty scaling operations without clear goals, tracking, and defined team roles, keeping them stuck in day-to-day sales tasks. The solution is to set specific goals and KPIs, monitor performance, and refine strategies, allowing founders to delegate and focus on the broader company strategy (Pillar Three).

In summary, wherever there is sales, there must be a problem-solution connection.

Create Your Connection

Keep these in mind as you determine your problem-solution connection.

1. Decide *what* problem you solve.

2. Define *who* you're solving the problem for.

3. Differentiate *how* your solution is better than the competition.

Bannerse: A Product Searching for a Problem

The first three years of tech startup Bannerse's development highlight the pitfalls of building a business around a product rather than around a problem.

Initially, co-founders Peter Strobel Tiborcz and Emi Farkas launched an interactive streaming platform during COVID-19, offering live and recorded fitness, health, and yoga content. The platform was popular during the pandemic but its appeal faded as life returned to normal, prompting the company to pivot.

They next explored the live-stream shopping trend in Asia, where consumers purchase goods through influencer-hosted events. Inspired by this, the founders applied their technology to introduce live-stream shopping in the West, only

> *"The first three years of Bannerse's development highlight the pitfalls of building a business around a product rather than around a problem."*

to find European agencies preferred traditional, polished campaigns over influencer-driven content. This forced them to rethink their approach again.

Pivoting once more, they retooled their technology to enhance digital advertising by embedding interactive elements like surveys and purchases directly into banner ads, keeping users engaged without redirecting them to a static page. Peter and Emi reached out to me for help in refining the problem-solution connection for this new iteration. Despite initial interest and brand partnerships, the solution didn't gain traction, with potential customers seeing it as a "nice to have" rather than a "must-have."

A Final Pivot?

Determined to find a viable problem-solution fit, Bannerse is now on its fourth iteration, focusing on the sports sector. Peter and Emi identified a key issue: marketing messages to sports fans during live events are often fragmented, with fans relying on multiple apps for information and purchases. To solve this, Bannerse is integrating all functions into a single QR code, providing a unified platform for fans to access information, interact, and make transactions, while offering advertisers a direct connection to potential customers. They aim to engage cricket, motorsport, and golf fans both at events and at home, enabling them to access content and make purchases during ad breaks.

Bannerse has made significant progress with each pivot, bringing them closer to a clear problem-solution connection. Now, target customers are reaching out, recognizing the potential in the sports sector. The shift from being a "nice to have" to gaining traction with major corporations signals a positive change.

Peter and Emi's key lesson from their journey is the importance of identifying a specific problem before developing a solution. As Peter puts it, "We had to accept that we were never solving an important problem. Instead, we had built a technology that was looking for a problem to solve. We've learned our lesson."

* * *

Key Takeaways

- **Sales is About Problem-Solving**: Sales is centered on identifying and addressing customers' specific problems, not on manipulation. A genuine problem-solving approach builds trust and leads to meaningful, lasting client relationships.

- **Define Your Niche and Specialize**: Focus narrowly on the specific problem you solve, who you solve it for, and how you solve it uniquely. Starting with a clear niche enables you to attract and serve ideal customers effectively and expand once your core offering is solid.

- **Finding Problem-Solution Fit Takes Time**: The journey often involves refining and pivoting until you find a clear problem-solution connection. Identifying a specific problem and aligning your solution to meet that need is crucial for taking a product from "nice to have" to "must-have."

PART 2

STRATEGIES

A common misconception among founders is that their product or market is so unique that traditional B2B sales and marketing strategies don't apply to them. While every founder believes their business is different, the truth is that the most effective strategies have been tested and proven across multiple industries.

Matteo Berlucchi, a serial entrepreneur who has launched nine businesses in verticals like real estate, media, e-commerce, and enterprise software, is currently the founder and CEO of Healthily, a healthcare platform. He knows firsthand that selling to business customers follows the same core principles, no matter what the vertical. "The key is understanding the psychology of the buyer," Matteo explains. "People buy in similar ways, regardless of the product. While each industry has its nuances, the commonalities far outweigh the differences."

Having mentored over 200 startups across a wide range of industries—including martech, fintech, edtech, agtech, healthtech, media, logistics, enterprise software, and organizational development—I've observed that founder-led sales organizations consistently encounter the same core challenges. First, customers must understand why they should buy what they're offering. Second, founders must clearly define their ideal customer and experiment with a structured mix of outbound sales, partnerships, and inbound marketing to reach them. Finally, as the business grows, founders need to scale their team so they can eventually step away from the daily sales grind and focus on long-term strategy and growth.

These three pillars—focus, structure, and scale—form the foundation of *The Launch Code*. In the chapters ahead, I'll break these pillars into nine distinct modules, each offering frameworks and actionable strategies that have empowered founders to accelerate their revenue growth.

Don't just read these chapters—apply their content to your business. Doing so will transform these insights and tools into measurable results.

THE LAUNCH CODE™

FOCUS

**YOUR OFFER
AND MESSAGE,
SO PROSPECTS
UNDERSTAND WHAT
YOU'RE SELLING**

VALUE PROPOSITION

PRODUCT OFFERING

MESSAGING & TOOLS

STRUCTURE

YOUR CLIENT
ACQUISITION,
SO YOU CLOSE MORE
DEALS WITH
LESS EFFORT

OUTBOUND SALES

PARTNERSHIPS

INBOUND MARKETING

SCALE

YOUR OPERATIONS,
SO YOU SUSTAIN
LONG-TERM GROWTH
AND EMPOWER
YOUR TEAM.

GOAL SETTING

PERFORMANCE TRACKING

TEAM DEVELOPMENT

CHAPTER 3

Focus Your Offer and Message

"People think focus means saying yes to the thing you've got to focus on. But... it means saying no to the hundred other good ideas."

– Steve Jobs

It was a chilly January evening in Budapest when I stepped onto the upper deck of A38, a decommissioned Ukrainian cargo vessel moored on the Pest side of the Danube River. In 2003, the ship was transformed into a cultural hotspot—a stylish bar, restaurant, exhibition hall, dance floor, and concert venue rolled into one. *Lonely Planet* readers once crowned A38 the "best bar in the world." On this night, it was the site of the Hungarian startup ecosystem's annual post-New Year's Eve gala, where I was set to receive the Startup Mentor of the Year award.

After the awards ceremony, I found myself leaning against an elegant wooden bar, watching the mingling crowd of founders, investors, and service providers. That's when he approached—a man in his mid-forties, sharply dressed in a sports coat, dress shirt, and jeans. He exuded confidence, but within moments, his polished exterior gave way to a string of clichés and misconceptions so outlandish they could have been lifted straight from a parody of tech culture.

With breathless enthusiasm, he declared that his startup had no direct competitors and was poised to disrupt tech giants like Facebook and Google. He explained that his team was in the final stages of product development and had secured intellectual property protections to fend off copycats. I stood there, wondering if he noticed me roll my eyes in thinly veiled skepticism.

Sensing the need to ground the conversation in reality, I asked a simple question: "Who are your target customers?" His answer was a masterclass in unfocused ambition: "We've picked five types of customers in each of five industries." He said this with such conviction that for a moment, I thought he might be joking. He wasn't.

It was then that I realized the hopelessness of our discussion. "Targeting so many markets at once is a recipe for disaster," I explained, attempting to inject some reason into the conversation. I outlined how dividing attention and resources across such a broad spectrum would only lead to inefficiency and, eventually, failure. But he waved off my concerns with a dismissive, "All we have to do now is sell," as though customer acquisition was a mere formality, easily checked off on his to-do list.

The founder's glaring lack of focus was impossible to overlook. Despite his eagerness, he couldn't clearly articulate what his company did or identify the problem it aimed to solve.

Embrace the Power of Focus

Don't mistake this story as proof that I'm wary of confident, ambitious entrepreneurs. I firmly believe in the power of setting bold, aspirational goals, like the €100 million revenue target I pursued at TV2. Ambition without clarity, however, is a recipe for failure. This founder's over-the-top attitude revealed a critical flaw: the inability to focus his limited time and resources on solving one problem exceptionally well and communicating his solution in a way that customers could immediately understand.

Focus is the cornerstone of a successful, sustainable business. It simplifies every stage of the entrepreneurial journey—from product development to sales, marketing, hiring, and even setting your daily to-do list. Having focus empowers you to develop your business in the desired direction, rather than wandering around aimlessly.

Finding your focus has tangible benefits. First, it helps you track your progress effectively by

"Focus is the cornerstone of a successful, sustainable business."

comparing your current position to your desired outcome, allowing for course corrections when needed. Second, it helps you make smarter, more informed decisions: Is this client the right fit? Does this partnership align with my goals? Should I prioritize one hire over another? With a clear focus, the answers become easier, if not self-evident.

Focusing Means Saying "No"

The hardest part of finding your focus is committing to it—saying "no" to seemingly promising opportunities that are out of focus. This can feel risky, especially for an early-stage, financially unstable business. For instance, why would you decline a paying client for a tangentially related product or service whose revenue might improve your bottom line? The reason is simple: while it may provide short-term income, diverting your time and resources risks compromising your long-term vision.

Apple co-founder Steve Jobs famously championed this principle. He regularly asked his executives what they had said "no" to today, emphasizing that focus isn't just about what you choose to pursue, but what you consciously decide to ignore. "People think focus means saying yes to the thing you've got to focus on," Jobs explained. "But that's not what it means at all. It means saying no to the hundred other good ideas that there are. You have to pick carefully."

Jobs used this mindset to transform Apple during his return to lead the company after a twelve-year hiatus. Facing financial collapse, he cut the company's product line by 70 percent, narrowing its focus to just four offerings: a desktop and a laptop for business users, and one each for consumers. This decision revitalized Apple. In his first fiscal year back, Apple lost $1.04 billion and teetered on the brink of bankruptcy. But the following year, the company turned a $309 million profit, laying the foundation for its ascent to becoming a global technology powerhouse.

Jobs's example underscores a vital truth: focus enables long-term success by aligning every decision and resource with your core goals. Saying "no" is often the most strategic choice you can make.

Tapping Into "The Law of Attraction"

There's a third, often overlooked benefit to narrowing your attention: it helps you recognize opportunities that align with your focus.

This principle is rooted in how our brains process information. When you focus on something specific, you train your mind to notice related details that might otherwise go unnoticed—a phenomenon psychologists call the frequency illusion, also referred to as "The Law of Attraction."

I experienced this phenomenon firsthand while shopping for a new car. After extensive research, I decided to buy a black Volkswagen Arteon. Suddenly, I started spotting black Volkswagen Arteons everywhere: in traffic, parked on streets, and passing me on highways. Of course, there weren't actually more of them on the road. My decision had simply attuned my brain to notice them.

The same principle applies to business. When you clarify your focus—whether it's a target market, a problem you're solving, or a specific goal—you naturally become more aware of opportunities that align with it. Your attention amplifies your ability to spot patterns, identify resources, and connect with people who support your vision.

The Launch Code: Pillar One

"Focus your offer and message" is the first pillar of *The Launch Code* and forms the foundation of your B2B sales and marketing strategy. This pillar helps you determine three critical aspects: what you communicate, to whom, and how. Mastering these naturally sets the stage for the second pillar, which reveals the process of reaching and acquiring customers.

To build a strong foundation, you need to get three components right:

1. **Value Proposition**: This explains what your business does and the unique value it delivers to your target clients. It's your answer to the question: "Why should someone buy what I'm selling?"

2. **Product Offering**: This is the solution you deliver, enabling customers to access the value outlined in your value proposition. Think of it as the practical means by which you address your customer's needs and fulfill their expectations.

3. **Client Messaging and Tools**: This is the communication you craft to engage your target audience. It spans your sales tools and marketing platforms, aiming to educate, persuade, and ultimately drive action.

These components are interconnected and getting them right ensures your efforts are aligned and impactful. Let's dive into each of these, one by one.

Module 1

Value Proposition

* * *

A value proposition is a concise statement that explains the problem you solve, who you solve it for, and why your solution is better than the competition. It distills your focus into a single sentence and emphasizes your problem-solution connection. Many tech founders and service providers struggle to clearly define their value proposition. Some wrestle with formulating one at all, while others ramble, overwhelming their audience in a flood of irrelevant details. Neither approach is effective.

"Your value proposition distills your focus into a single sentence and emphasizes your problem-solution connection."

Think of a company without a clear value proposition as a rudderless boat—it may float, but it will drift aimlessly, with no clear direction. A business with an unclear value proposition faces scattered product development, unclear marketing messages, and unpredictable sales results. This often leads to frustration and can even make founders reluctant to engage in sales and marketing at all.

Creating a value proposition isn't as difficult as it may seem. I've worked with early-stage founders who were initially baffled by the concept. Yet, in just forty-five minutes, we developed a value proposition they could use effectively in conversations, emails, and on their websites. In some cases, this exercise has been transformative.

For example, I once worked with the founders of a social media analytics startup that helped corporations understand their customers' hidden motivations by analyzing online chats and text in over thirty languages. Despite their strong product, their value proposition was unclear, and even the company's founders struggled to explain what their company did. We worked together to clarify their value proposition, which transformed how they communicated internally and externally.

The results were immediate. They began closing deals consistently, generating predictable income, and hitting revenue milestones that unlocked additional funding. Within a year, the company was recognized as one of the top three most promising startups in their market. More importantly, the founders gained clarity and peace of mind.

Bence Badinszky, co-founder of a fintech startup Payee, had a similar experience when he applied this approach to clarifying his company's value proposition: "I felt there was a lot of confusion, but now I can articulate the right problem and how we solve it. We've come a long way. I finally feel in control of my company."

Read Yours in Ten Seconds

In this section, I'll show you how to create your value proposition by breaking it down into its component parts and reassembling them into a single, coherent sentence. This will allow you to explain your business clearly in eight to ten seconds, immediately capturing your target audience's attention.

Let's start by examining the value propositions of some well-known businesses.

Here's Facebook's: "Facebook is a social media platform that helps people to communicate more efficiently with their friends, family, and coworkers by connecting them through an easy-to-use online platform."

Now, Salesforce: "Salesforce is a customer management platform that helps businesses to improve their sales results by collecting and analyzing client information and creating quality sales management processes."

Uber has two different value propositions: one for users and one for drivers. For users: "Uber is a car-sharing service that helps city residents to travel conveniently, twenty-four hours a day, seven days a week, by calling a ride with one click, and tracking the driver."

For drivers: "Uber is a car-sharing service that helps automobile owners to earn income using their vehicle to transport passengers by making their availability visible to potential customers."

You'll notice that Uber's value propositions are targeted toward two distinct groups, highlighting their different needs. Your business might face a similar challenge, needing to address both end customers and resellers. In such cases, it's crucial to craft distinct value propositions for each group. Avoid creating multiple value propositions for the same audience, however, as this can lead to confusion and dilute your message.

5 Steps to Create a Value Proposition

As you go through this framework, keep in mind that solutions that directly increase your customer's revenue or cut costs are easier to sell than those that are merely nice to have. The latter, like products that build brand awareness or improve employee satisfaction, are important but carry less sense of urgency. They are also put on the back burner during tough economic times.

> *"Solutions that directly increase your customer's revenue or cut costs are easier to sell than those that are merely nice to have."*

Let's go through each step:

1. **Customer problem/need**: *What problem does my business solve or need does it fulfill?*

   Write a series of statements, *expressed in the voice of your customer*, that start with a phrase like, "I need…" or "I wish I could…" or "I must have…" List as many problems as you can to start; you will narrow these down later.

2. **Target customer**: *What type of company will buy my solution?*

   Start by considering relevant client characteristics like company size, industry, or location. For instance, you might target telecommunications companies with 2,000 to 5,000 employees in Southern Europe. Next, identify the job titles of the decision-makers or influencers you need to reach.

3. **Product/Service description**: *What do I call my product or service?*

Describe your product or service in three or four words that your target client can easily understand. For example, you might be a "customer loyalty platform," a "video production studio," or a "pest control technology." Keep it simple and avoid buzzwords.

4. **Key benefit**: *How will my target customer benefit most from using my product or service?*

Identify all the benefits your product or service offers to your target client. Many of these will directly address the problems identified in step one, while others may be more emotional, like "providing clarity" or "boosting self-confidence." Select the most impactful benefit from your list to highlight as your key benefit. Try to stick to just one.

5. **Competitive advantage**: *What makes my product or service unique or more compelling than other alternatives?*

Consider why customers should choose your solution over others. List all your competitive advantages, then focus on the most important one. This is often *how* you deliver your solution—your unique process, system, or a benefit you didn't select as your key benefit.

A strong competitive advantage should be *meaningful* (relevant to your customer), *deliverable* (something you can reliably provide), and *defendable* (something competitors can't easily replicate).

Avoid using price as your competitive advantage since rivals can simply undercut you and drive you toward rapid decline.

Putting the Pieces Together

Distill each of your answers into a single thought or sentence. Keep these as simple as possible as you'll be using them to create your single-sentence value proposition.

I'll show you how my client, Povio, a software development firm, used this process to position itself as a top choice for enterprise clients.

Their summary answers looked like this:

- **Problem/need** (expressed from the *client's point of view*): "I lack the internal engineering talent to deliver the software to support my core business on time and on budget."

- **Target customer**: Hardware manufacturers without a "software culture"

- **Product/Service description**: Software development firm

- **Key benefit**: Accelerate stagnant software projects

- **Competitive advantage**: Augment internal teams with high-quality engineers

Next, they slotted their answers into my standard value proposition format:

[Company name] is a [product/service definition] that helps [target customer] to [key benefit] by [competitive advantage].

This generated the following sentence:

"Povio is a software development firm that helps hardware manufacturers without a 'software culture' to accelerate stagnant software projects by augment internal teams with high-quality engineers."

This was close, but not perfect.

They felt that customers might not appreciate the reference to lacking a software culture, so they took that out. For grammatical reasons, they altered "augment" to "augmenting". Finally, they decided they needed to make their competitive advantage more specific so clients could understand Povio's unique skills, so they changed it to "augmenting internal teams with expert engineers who optimize infrastructure and workflow."

This was their final value proposition statement:

"Povio is a software development firm that helps hardware manufacturers to accelerate stagnant software projects by augmenting internal teams with expert engineers who optimize infrastructure and workflow."

Pretty clear, huh?

Jakob Cvetco, co-founder of Povio, recalls the impact that applying this framework had on clarifying their customer communication: "This process guided us through highly specific questions, and helped us piece everything together to develop a powerful, effective value proposition."

Now it's your turn.

Value Proposition Dos and Don'ts

Keep these points in mind as you create your value proposition.

Dos

- Make sure it's focused

- Test it and revise it based on feedback

- Understand that getting it right is a process

Don'ts

- Highlight features (what you can do) without benefits (why clients should care)

- Define your target customer too broadly

- Fill it with industry jargon

* * *

Key Takeaways

- **A Value Proposition Creates Clarity**: A strong value proposition defines the problem you solve, who you solve it for, and why your solution is better. It helps founders build confidence, align their team, and set a clear direction for growth.

- **Make Your Value Proposition Simple**: Make sure your value proposition is simple, focused, and easily understandable within eight to ten seconds. Don't create multiple value propositions for a single audience segment.

- **5-Step Process to Create a Value Proposition**: Start by defining the customer problem, identifying your target audience, summarizing your product, highlighting the key benefit, and emphasizing your unique competitive advantage. Apply your answers to a standardized sentence structure to create a high-impact value proposition.

Module 2

Product Offering

* * *

To transform your product or service into a successful business, you must present your value proposition in a way that customers can easily understand and say "yes" to. This is your product offering.

At first glance, some founders might find this concept straightforward, thinking, "I'm a digital marketer, so I offer digital marketing." While that's technically correct, it's only part of the story. There are countless ways to structure and deliver such a service. The key is ensuring your target customer knows exactly how to access your solution.

Consider this analogy: imagine you're an artist. You have several ways to offer your work:

- **Exclusive and high value**: Sell individual paintings at premium prices through an art gallery.

- **Accessible and scalable:** Offer reproductions as posters, making them affordable and available in stores or as digital downloads.

- **Diverse and customizable**: Set up a website where customers can buy your artwork printed on items like mugs, t-shirts, or mouse pads.

Each approach shares your art, but targets different customers, price points, and sales channels.

Your product offering rests on three core pillars: your business model, packaging, and pricing. How you design and balance these elements determines how successfully you attract and retain customers—and, ultimately, your business's growth.

Confirm Your Business Model

Are you selling physical products, services, or a mix of both?

For physical products, set a price above production and distribution costs to generate profit, selling

> *"Your product offering rests on three core pillars: your business model, packaging, and pricing."*

directly or through distributors. For services, factor in your time, technology, and overhead, adding a profit margin. Services can be offered on a project basis or through ongoing contracts for recurring revenue. A hybrid model combines products with complementary services, like setup or maintenance, diversifying revenue streams and providing stability, especially in uncertain times.

Here are some common business models:

- **Subscription**: Charge a recurring fee for ongoing access to your product or service. For cloud-based software (SaaS), the software is the product, but its access is delivered as a service.

It provides predictable revenue streams and encourages long-term customer relationships. Examples: Netflix, Salesforce.

- **Freemium**: Offer a basic version of your product or service for free, with an option to upgrade to a premium version for more features. This differs from a free trial, which provides full access for a limited time. This model attracts a large user base and converts free users into paying customers over time. Examples: MailChimp, LinkedIn.

- **Single Payment**: Customers pay once for lifetime access. Best used for products or services with lasting value, such as software, hardware, or digital content. Revenue is one-time, making it less predictable compared to recurring models. Examples: Apple, Udemy, and SaaS tools offering unlimited-use options.

- **Marketplace**: A platform that connects buyers and sellers, earning revenue through commissions on sales or by offering additional services (e.g., insurance, advertising). It's scalable, as the business facilitates transactions rather than owning inventory. Examples: Alibaba, eBay.

- **Franchise/Licensing**: License your brand, business model, or technology to others. The licensee manages local operations, while the parent company earns fees or royalties. This model enables scalability without direct operational oversight. Examples: NVIDIA (license), McDonald's (franchise).

- **Professional Services**: Charge for specialized services related to your core product, such as onboarding, training, or technical support. It helps customers implement complex enterprise software while generating additional revenue, but requires skilled personnel, which may limit growth potential. Examples: SAP, Oracle.

While all these business models are valid, the most successful ones generate recurring revenue and are scalable. Recurring sales offer predictability, ensuring stable revenue, while scalability allows growth with minimal cost increases, enhancing profitability.

Investors favor businesses with these attributes because, with effective management, they can grow rapidly. This is why the SaaS business model has become so popular among tech startups over the past decade.

Offer Choices, but Not Too Many

Your goal should be to provide clients with enough options to feel in control, but not so many that they become overwhelmed. Striking this balance is essential for facilitating decisions and boosting customer satisfaction.

"The most successful business models generate recurring revenue and are scalable."

Think back to the last time you went to a supermarket for toothpaste. Instead of a simple choice, you were confronted with dozens of options: whitening, fluoride-free, sensitive-teeth formulas, all from different brands and sizes. What should have been an easy decision became overwhelming.

For low-cost, everyday items like toothpaste, you likely default to a familiar option. But for higher-ticket or non-essential products and services, too many choices can lead to decision paralysis. A confused mind never buys.

On the opposite end, consider Henry Ford's famous offer for the Model T: customers could choose "any color [they] want, as long as it's black." While this simplicity helped Ford in his time, it also eliminated the customer's sense of autonomy. Most early-stage businesses don't have this luxury.

The ideal approach is to offer three standard choices. This strategy strikes a balance; it gives clients a sense of control without creating confusion. It also leverages psychology by recognizing that people are more confident in their decisions when given a limited, manageable set of options. You will accelerate the sales process and increase the likelihood of successfully closing deals.

Packaging Your Offer

The most common packaging strategies are *Tiers*, *Stages*, and *Categories*. Each divides

"A confused mind never buys."

your product or service into three options, varying in features like capacity, users, functionality, reporting and support. They differ in how these choices are structured and how they relate to one another.

Tiers

The Tiers strategy organizes product features into three levels: basic, standard, and premium. You can label these tiers however you like, perhaps Bronze, Silver, Gold, or Essentials, Professional, Enterprise. The core idea is that each tier offers increasingly higher quality or additional features.

- **Basic**: This entry-level option provides essential features at a lower price, catering to budget-conscious clients or those with minimal needs.

- **Standard**: Positioned as the most balanced option, this tier offers a good mix of features and value, making it the optimal choice for most customers.

- **Premium**: This top-tier option includes the highest level of features and services at a premium price, targeting customers who want the best and are willing to pay for extra benefits.

In practice, 75–85 percent of customers will gravitate toward the middle option. It feels like the safest, most familiar choice—the "just right" selection, as Goldilocks would say.

Stages

The Stages strategy creates a progression, where each option builds on the previous one. Clients start with the entry-level service and move to higher levels as they progress. This strategy works particularly well for service providers who need to assess a client's needs before offering a comprehensive solution.

> *"In practice, 75–85 percent of customers will gravitate toward the middle option."*

- **Entry-Level**: Start with a basic, low-cost service that builds trust and demonstrates value. Examples include initial consultations, basic audits, or preliminary reports. This stage should deliver measurable value and kick-start the client relationship.

- **Mid-Level**: The next stage offers more in-depth solutions, building on the entry-level service. It could include comprehensive strategy development, extended diagnostics, or more complex implementation services.

- **High-Level**: The highest stage provides the most extensive and complete service, often including ongoing support or advanced features. This stage represents the culmination of the client relationship and targets those seeking the full benefit of your offering.

While it may be tempting to offer your entry-level service for free to build trust, *avoid giving it away*. Offering it for free can devalue your service and waste time and resources. In my experience, clients rarely appreciate free offerings, so only consider this approach if you're confident it will eventually lead to a significant financial return.

Categories

The Categories strategy organizes your services or products into three distinct groups based on relevance rather than service level. This approach helps clients focus on what's most appropriate for their needs, preventing them from feeling overwhelmed by too many options.

Organize your services or products into categories that align with your business and client requirements. For instance, a fitness business might organize services into age groups (18–29, 30–45, 46+) or exercise types (strength training, cardio, flexibility).

If you find it difficult to define three distinct categories, it may be a sign that you need to narrow your focus and simplify your offering. As

I often remind founders, "If you're everything to everybody, you're nothing to nobody."

Fine Tune Your Product Offering

Here are some things to keep in mind as you work on your product offering.

Testing and Adjusting: It may take several iterations to finalize your product offering. You might need to test different distributions of features and services across your three options until you find a structure that resonates with your target customers. It's also possible that you'll need to shift strategies, such as moving from Tiers to Stages.

Avoid over-testing. Instead, aim to quickly establish a minimum viable product offering. You can always refine and adjust as you go. It's better to have a starting point than to begin each sales conversation with a blank slate.

Avoid Custom Proposals: While it may seem customer-focused, tailoring proposals for each client lengthens the sales cycle. Prospects may take months to decide, and you'll spend a lot of time crafting tailored proposals. It will also make scaling difficult. Standardizing your packages streamlines the process, reduces decision-making time, and saves you effort.

Steve Ruszina, co-founder of Invention Factory, applied this principle to his organizational development consultancy and saw immediate results. "I managed to package my products into various portfolios, allowing customers to choose the one that best fits their needs. This made it easier for them to navigate and select their preferred path. That was a game changer for me."

In summary, offering a limited but well-defined set of choices, using effective packaging strategies, and standardizing your approach will simplify decision-making for your clients and make your sales process more efficient.

Offer Packaging Examples

Try one of these product offering strategies, so you make it easy for your prospect to say "yes" to your offer.

Tiers

Syndicast is a SaaS platform that helps music labels promote new releases to streaming services and radio stations worldwide. They offer three service tiers: Standard, Plus, and Pro. Each tier delivers a longer promo period, more tools, and more detailed reporting.

Stages

Computomics uses AI to help agricultural companies breed market-ready crops faster. They start with an entry-level service (BreedScope) to assess a client's breeding program. After that, clients can choose either a standard service (xSeedScore) for crop predictions or a premium option (xSeedScore Plus) that includes a dedicated analyst.

Categories

Logiscool is a network of coding schools for kids aged six to seventeen. They offer educational content like digital discovery, programming, and robotics, in three formats: semester courses, summer camps, and workshops. Kids and parents first choose the learning format, then select the topic and appropriate skill level.

How to Set Your Pricing

Pricing your product or service is challenging because it mixes economics and psychology. Your goal is to maximize profit while ensuring that customers see the value in your offer. Setting the right price requires you to align your costs, your perceived value, and the competitive landscape.

Follow these guidelines:

Start with Target Profit: Calculate costs associated with creating, marketing, and delivering your product or service—this includes labor, materials, and operating expenses. Then, determine your target profit margin. For low-cost, high-volume products, your margin might be 5–10 percent, whereas for premium services you

> *"Pricing your product or service is challenging because it mixes economics and psychology."*

could aim for 60–80 percent. To attract customers, you might initially offer your product at a low profit margin, but avoid this in the long run. Poor unit economics—selling at a loss—means your business won't last.

Understand Perceived Value: The perceived value of your product or service is crucial. Fashion, automotive, and luxury goods brands regularly price based on their brand's reputation. That's why Chanel can charge $600 for a steel keychain. In B2B, customers judge pricing by the value you deliver. If you charge €100 to fix a €10 problem, it seems overpriced. But if you charge €10 to solve a €100 problem, it looks like great value.

Research the Competition: Investigate how much competitors charge for similar offerings. While it might be tempting to place yourself somewhere in the middle, this can land you squarely in "no-man's land," where you don't stand out. Instead, consider positioning yourself as either a high-value, low-cost provider or a premium option.

Set Pricing that Supports the Middle Option: When offering different service levels, use a 70/100/170 pricing ratio. For instance, if your middle-tier service is priced at 100, price your entry-level option at 70 and your premium option at 170. This strategy helps make the middle option appear to offer the best value—better than the entry-level option while still more affordable than the premium option.

Reflect and Adjust: Before finalizing your price, consider raising it by an additional 10 percent. Initial doubts about the value of your service will likely lead you to price your product too low. As you gather customer testimonials and demand increases, however, justifying higher prices becomes psychologically easier.

Adapt Based on Market Feedback: Ultimately, market response will determine whether your pricing is right. If your product is selling well, your pricing strategy is likely on track. If not, seek feedback, adjust, and test again. Pricing is not a one-time decision; it requires ongoing flexibility and willingness to adapt to changing circumstances.

* * *

Key Takeaways

- **Make Your Offering Easy to Understand**: Your product offering defines how customers access your solution. Offering the same service in different ways can appeal to various customer segments. A clear, well-structured offering tailored to your audience boosts sales potential.

- **Three Elements Shape Your Product Offering**: Your product offering is defined by three key factors: business model, packaging, and pricing. Effectively balancing these will attract clients and support sustainable growth, with recurring and scalable models often yielding the best results.

- **Provide Enough Choices Without Overwhelming**: To avoid sparking decision paralysis, offer clients three options across different tiers, stages, or categories. This simplifies their choice, boosts satisfaction, and speeds up the sales process. Too many options can confuse, while too few may feel limiting.

Client Messaging and Tools

* * *

With your value proposition and product offering ready, the final step is to present them in a way that grabs attention and inspires action. Effective messaging doesn't just explain what your product does—it demonstrates how you solve a pressing problem, shows customers how they can benefit from and access your solution, and builds trust every step of the way.

This is the essence of customer-first messaging.

Many founders fall into the trap of focusing too much on their product's features instead of the value it delivers. No matter how innovative your technology is, prospects care most about how it benefits them. Take the example of a Porsche—people don't buy one just for its impeccable engineering; its status and the lifestyle it

"Your prospects will care about who you are only after they clearly understand the problem you solve and the value you deliver."

promises is what seals the deal. Your prospects will care about who you are only after they clearly understand the problem you solve and the value you deliver.

Once your messaging framework is ready, apply it consistently across all your communication channels—emails, websites, social media, and pitch decks—to ensure a unified and compelling narrative.

Messaging Framework Building Blocks

Your messaging framework is composed of six key elements that work together to deliver a clear and compelling narrative. Some will draw from your existing value proposition and product details, while others will require fresh development.

These building blocks are:

1. **Desired Outcome**: *This is the feeling or result your target customer hopes to achieve once their problem is solved.*

   Think of it as a headline that captures their dreams. For example:

   - "Videos your customers will love." [business video producer]

   - "A sold-out show every time." [dynamic ticket pricing technology]

   - "A product launch on time, on budget." [software development firm]

   - "Access to all your data in a usable form." [database management platform]

   Your desired outcome should focus on what your audience wants, without directly mentioning your product or service. It should grab their attention and make them think "I want that," even before they know how you'll deliver it. Keep it clear and compelling—if it's unclear or vague, prospects will lose interest.

2. **Customer Problem or Need**: *This is the issue your business addresses.*

   Use the problem statement you created for your value proposition.

3. **Your Solution**: *Describe how your business solves the problem mentioned above.*

   This should be your value proposition.

4. **Call to Action**: *Clearly state the action you want your target customer to take.*

   When prospects find your solution relevant, they'll be ready to act. Provide clear instructions on how they can engage with your product or service—whether it's scheduling a meeting, downloading content, or signing up for a webinar. Include an easy-to-find link, button, form, email, or phone number to facilitate their next step.

5. **Credibility Builders**: *Include elements that build trust and confidence in your solution.*

   You may need to offer extra reassurance before your prospect is ready to take action. Tap into these credibility builders:

   - *Social Proof:* Display logos of past clients, customer testimonials, or industry awards.

   - *Implementation Plan:* Explain exactly how you'll deliver your solution. For example:

- Step 1: Evaluate your existing data.
- Step 2: Tailor our solution to your tech stack.
- Step 3: Implement our system in two weeks.

- *Product Offering:* Present your offer clearly, outlining options without overwhelming prospects with excessive details. If you have fixed prices or a "click and buy" option, include the costs. Publishing pricing can also help filter out customers who may not be able to afford your services.

6. **Key Benefits**: *Highlight both rational and emotional benefits of your solution.*
   Combine practical benefits, such as cost savings, with emotional ones, such as peace of mind. Highlight the key benefit from your value proposition and add two or three additional advantages that make your offer more appealing.

Bring Your Messaging Framework to Life

Follow these tips to guide you as you develop your messaging framework:

Use Simple, Clear Language: Ensure your copy is straightforward and easy to understand, even for an intelligent twelve-year-old. Avoid jargon and buzzwords, as clarity is key to keeping your prospects engaged. Even the most tech-savvy customer, attuned to industry-specific terminology, will respond better to a simple, easily grasped message.

Address People, Not Just Companies: Focus on the individuals within the companies you're targeting. Speak to their emotions, needs, and concerns. Using engaging headlines or humor helps build a connection, making prospects more likely to respond.

Write Copy That Sells: Be persuasive. Highlight the specific impact of your product. Instead of simply stating that your solution "generates revenue," say it can "10x your growth in 90 days." Instead of simply "reducing costs," highlight how it "frees up cash to invest in what matters most." Frame benefits in a way that excites and motivates prospects to take action.

Stay Consistent Across Platforms: Apply your messaging framework consistently across all platforms and tools. Use the same logos, fonts, colors, and icons to make your marketing instantly

"Avoid jargon and buzzwords, as clarity is key to keeping your prospects engaged."

recognizable. Consistency makes your brand memorable, increases engagement, and builds trust, while keeping your name top of mind for prospects.

How to Apply Your Messaging

The core building blocks of your framework remain the same, but you'll need to tailor them for each messaging tool and platform to ensure maximum impact. This will ensure you have materials on hand that you can integrate into your daily sales activities. As Radek Novotny, co-founder of AI automation startup Superface, puts it, "I use these messaging tools at least twice a week to craft clear, market-ready communication through one-pagers and emails."

Here's how to adapt your framework for different contexts.

Emails

When writing your emails, start by focusing on the problem your target customer faces, not a long introduction about yourself. For example, begin with something like, "Logistics managers like you struggle with tracking warehouse inventory" and then explain how your solution addresses it. This shifts the focus to customer needs.

Always include a clear call to action, such as "Let's schedule a call," "Click to book a demo," or "Reply if you're interested."

In follow-up emails, vary your opening sentence by emphasizing the prospect's desired outcome, such as "Imagine knowing your customer data is secure." Add credibility through customer logos, testimonials, or awards to build trust.

Craft engaging subject lines to encourage opens. Avoid vague subjects like "software development services." Instead, use up to ten words to:

- Describe their desired outcome.

- Mention a referral (e.g., "Joe Smith suggested we speak").

- Highlight a key benefit (e.g., "Save 30 percent on your marketing costs").

Website Homepage and Sales Sheet

Apply the messaging framework to your website's homepage and your sales sheet in the same way, adjusting only for space constraints.

- **Headline**: Reflect your client's desired outcome. *"Achieve Effortless Inventory Management and Save Costs."*

- **Subheadline**: Present your value proposition concisely. *"We help logistics managers streamline operations and reduce tracking errors with our AI-powered solution."*

- **Three Key Benefits**: List them clearly beneath the subheadline.

  - Cut warehouse management costs by 30 percent
  - Enhance tracking precision with live updates
  - Integrate quickly with minimal disruption

- **Problem Section**: Describe the pain points your target customer faces. *"Warehouse managers are overwhelmed by inventory errors, inefficient systems, and costly delays."*

- **Solution Section**: Explain how your product solves the problem. *"Our solution uses AI to automate tracking, offering accurate, real-time data for better decision-making."*

- **Call to Action**: Make it clear and actionable. *"Schedule a demo to see how we can streamline your operations!"*

- **Social Proof**: Add testimonials, customer logos, or awards to build credibility. *"Trusted by over 200 logistics companies worldwide."*

- **Implementation Plan**: Explain exactly how you'll deliver your solution.

  - Step 1: Align goals via a kickoff call.
  - Step 2: Implement and integrate with existing systems.
  - Step 3: Provide training for your team.

- **Product Offering**: Briefly highlight your packages and prices, if applicable.

- **Key Benefits**: Remind prospects of the key benefits using slightly different wording.

Use bold headlines for each section to help people who only skim the page grasp key information quickly. Incorporate visuals such as customer photos, product images, and company logos to reinforce your message and build credibility. Adjust the content for the available space and format of each platform while maintaining the core structure.

Pitch Deck

Your pitch deck should be ten to fifteen slides long, each with a headline and three to four bullet points to support your narrative. Include visuals to enhance your message and keep the presentation within ten to fifteen minutes, allowing time for introductions, Q&A, and next steps. Structure the deck into three sections:

- **Customer Problem**: Clearly define the problem you solve (*customer problem or need*) and explain the potential risks of not addressing it right away. This highlights the urgency of the issue and sets the stage for introducing your solution.

- **Our Solution**: Describe your product or service by highlighting your value proposition (*your solution*) and explain how it works (*implementation plan*). Support claims with client testimonials or case studies (*social proof*).

- **Working Together**: Present your offer (*product offering*), emphasize the benefits customers gain (*key benefits*), and outline the next steps to take advantage of your offer (*call to action*).

Social Media

Create profiles on relevant social media platforms for yourself and your company. Design tailored cover banners for each profile with consistent visual elements from your website. Include your customer's desired outcome, your value proposition, and call to action in these banners. Ensure your profile descriptions align with your messaging framework.

Elevator Pitch

Develop three versions of your elevator pitch with varying lengths. The ten-second pitch should be your one-sentence value proposition. The twenty-second pitch should expand on this by including additional details about your product offering and possibly the implementation plan. The thirty-second pitch should incorporate social proof, such as client successes or a case study. In each case, end with a clear call to action if relevant. Practice delivering each pitch until they feel natural and conversational.

Client Messaging Tools & Platforms

Use these sales and marketing materials to reach, communicate, and engage with your target customers.

Emails: A series of three to five emails that introduce your product or service and aim to schedule a call or meeting. Each email builds on the previous one, adapting based on whether you receive a response.

Sales Sheet: A concise, one- to two-page overview of your business, also known as a "one-pager." It can be attached to an email or shared via a link.

Website: Your main hub for information about your business, often used as a landing page for your digital marketing efforts.

Pitch Deck: A presentation for pitching your business, used in personal or virtual meetings.

Social Media: Personal and business profiles on platforms relevant to B2B customers like LinkedIn, Facebook, YouTube, Instagram, and X (Twitter).

Elevator Pitch: A brief introduction to your business used during networking opportunities, prepared in 10-, 20-, and 30-second versions.

Key Takeaways

- **Customer-First Messaging Framework**: Focus on how your product solves a relevant problem, include a clear call to action, and build trust with your audience. This approach highlights your solution's value before diving into explaining your technology or product features.

- **Key Messaging Elements**: Your framework should include the desired outcome, the customer problem, solution, call to action, credibility builders, and key benefits. These elements combine to create a persuasive narrative that engages prospects.

- **Consistent Application Across Platforms**: Apply your messaging framework consistently across emails, websites, sales sheets, and social media. This reinforces your brand and ensures your message resonates at multiple touchpoints.

Focus Sharpens Over Time

* * *

Finding your focus takes patience.

It starts with drafting a value proposition, product offering, and client messaging using research, intuition, and common sense. This kicks off an iterative process: test your drafts

> *"Your focus is never really 'done'; it's just at a different stage of imperfect."*

with prospects, gather feedback, and refine your sales and marketing tools. Over time, this feedback loop continues until, like a puzzle, the pieces click into place.

This process is neither glamorous nor easy. For instance, DOQSYS, a procurement advisory firm, went through five versions of its value proposition before finding one that resonated with target customers. Similarly, Emed4all, a medical diagnostics startup, continually refined its product offering to align with customer needs. As I often tell clients: "Your focus is never really 'done'; it's just at a different stage of imperfect."

Unfortunately, AI tools and marketing platforms can't circumvent this process. True focus comes from integrating feedback from real sales interactions. It's through these experiences that you learn to say the right thing to the right prospect.

You'll know you've found your focus when your sales and marketing efforts start to flow seamlessly. Fewer objections, shorter sales cycles, better customers, and higher prices—all achieved with less effort.

Sounds awesome, right?

The clarity that comes with identifying your focus is transformative. When founders I work with refine their value proposition and messaging, they visibly relax, smile, and light up with ideas. They're energized by the positive ripple effects on their product, sales, and team. The confidence it brings is so powerful, I wish I could bottle it and sell it.

Vicket: Fix Your Focus to Grow

Vicket is a video streaming platform that helps sports teams record, analyze, and broadcast games. Today, it solves a key problem for a specific type of customer, but this was not always the case.

Originally named Live Event, the company tried to stream a wide variety of events—sports, concerts, even city council meetings—on one platform. Mixing ice hockey with political debates, however, confused potential customers. As co-founder Zsolt Nagy puts it, "We tried to solve every problem related to live streaming, but our mix of content created confusion. It was a complete mess."

When we started working together, we refocused Vicket's offer and message. The core value proposition became clear: automated video production technology specifically for sports teams. This allowed teams to record training sessions and matches, broadcast games to fans, and make real-time tactical adjustments.

This new focus paid off quickly. During a sales pitch to the Romanian football academy FC Csikszereda, Zsolt changed tactics. Instead of overwhelming the decision-makers with product features, Zsolt asked questions about the coaches' needs, tailoring his presentation to what mattered most to them. The coaches tested the platform on the spot and were impressed by its ease of use and the speed at which they could produce and analyze video, compared with the slow, cumbersome USB-based system they had been using thus far.

Zsolt then presented three tiers of service, and the club chose the highest one, resulting in Vicket's largest ever deal, which they closed at a follow-up meeting.

This shift in focus fueled rapid growth. Vicket has expanded from serving two ice hockey clubs in Romania to working with two dozen clients, including two sports federations. Now, the company plans to expand into new European markets and target basketball and soccer teams as well.

For Vicket, finding their focus wasn't just a strategy—it was the key to unlocking their success.

THE LAUNCH CODE™

FOCUS

YOUR OFFER
AND MESSAGE,
SO PROSPECTS
UNDERSTAND WHAT
YOU'RE SELLING

1 VALUE PROPOSITION

2 PRODUCT OFFERING

3 MESSAGING & TOOLS

STRUCTURE

YOUR CLIENT
ACQUISITION,
SO YOU CLOSE MORE
DEALS WITH
LESS EFFORT

1 OUTBOUND SALES

 2 PARTNERSHIPS

 3 INBOUND MARKETING

SCALE

YOUR OPERATIONS,
SO YOU SUSTAIN
LONG-TERM GROWTH
AND EMPOWER
YOUR TEAM.

1 GOAL SETTING

2 PERFORMANCE TRACKING

3 TEAM DEVELOPMENT

Structure Your Client Acquisition

"Sales without a strategy is like throwing spaghetti at the wall and hoping something sticks."

– Anonymous

Povio's journey mirrors the path of many founder-led businesses, whether in tech or professional services. Early on, these companies rely heavily on their networks, using personal relationships and referrals to secure their first clients. While this works in the beginning, they eventually hit a ceiling and find that network-based selling alone cannot scale. This forces them to seek a more structured, multi-channel approach to client acquisition.

Povio, launched in 2014 by Slovenian co-founders Matevz Petek and Jakob Cvetko, started as a photo-sharing app that allowed images to disappear. After joining Silicon Valley's Y Combinator, they quickly realized they couldn't compete with Snapchat and pivoted. With strong

101

engineering talent but no clear direction, Povio turned to its YC network, securing its first clients and generating millions in revenue through word-of-mouth referrals.

But as the company grew, Povio hit a revenue ceiling. Relying solely on referrals couldn't sustain their expanding team. The situation worsened during COVID-19 when they lost three key clients overnight. Cold emailing and a new website brought minimal results, leaving them without a consistent client acquisition system.

"We didn't have a reliable way of replacing clients when they left us," Jakob recalls. "We were just sitting here waiting for something to happen."

That's when Povio adopted *The Launch Code* and shifted to a proactive, structured approach to sales. They maximized revenue from existing clients through strong account management, while diversifying their sales strategy to include outbound sales, partnerships, and inbound marketing.

Povio's head of sales, Vid Lesnic, spearheaded these efforts, using personalized outreach via LinkedIn and email and building partnerships with venture capital firms and design agencies. They also created a marketing department focused on search engine optimization (SEO), content marketing, and digital advertising.

The results were clear: increased email open rates, higher-quality leads, and more clients. "We've gone from being a 'feelings-driven' to a 'data-driven' sales organization," Vid explains.

This strategic shift helped Povio grow to over $20 million in annual revenue and build a scalable, resilient business positioned for long-term growth.

Let's dive into how you can achieve this same result.

Your Ideal Customer is Your Bullseye

Building a revenue growth engine requires a proactive, structured approach to client acquisition from the start. Imagine trying to hit a target with a blindfold on—that's how it feels when you rely on a disorganized mix of network-based referrals or thousands of cold emails. On the other hand, a well-defined plan streamlines your efforts, driving faster, more predictable growth. The cornerstone of a structured approach is answering one critical question: *Who is most likely to buy what I'm selling?*

Your Ideal Customer Profile (ICP) is the "bullseye" that ensures your sales and marketing efforts are focused on the right prospects. It's a detailed portrait of the individuals or companies most likely to benefit from, consider, and ultimately purchase your offering. Focusing on your ICP doesn't *guarantee* a sale, but it significantly increases your chances. By defining your ICP, you can concentrate your resources on targeting the most relevant individuals or companies, making your efforts more effective and efficient.

> *"The cornerstone of a structured approach is answering one critical question: who is most likely to buy what I'm selling?"*

It also means you engage with fewer, but higher-quality prospects. Typically, the closing rate—the ratio of deals closed to qualified leads—hovers around 10–15 percent. By targeting your ICP, this can rise to 30 percent or higher, allowing you to close more deals with less effort, driving more scalable growth.

Identifying Your ICP

You already outlined the key traits of your target customer in your value proposition. Now, it's time to dive deeper and identify the specific qualities and behaviors that truly define your *ideal* customer. Think of your earlier description as a rough sketch, and this next step as creating a detailed, full-color likeness. The more precise your ICP, the easier it will be to identify and target the right companies.

Cover these four areas:

1. **General Characteristics:** *Describe your ideal customer in broad terms.*

   - What products or services do they offer?

   - How large are they in terms of employees or revenue?

   - How are they structured?

   - What are their buying behaviors?

   - Where are they located?

   If you're just starting out, with no clients—or only a few—make some basic assumptions. If you already have at least five satisfied customers who are a good fit for your business, look for characteristics they share. This can give you a solid foundation for crafting a more accurate and detailed ICP.

2. **Industry Focus:** *List the industries in which your ideal customer operates.*

   Industry definitions can be broad (e.g., financial services) or narrow (e.g., local banks)—the more specific, the better. Once you've listed all industries, rank them in order of relevance and/or importance. Explain why you chose these industries and what determined their ranking.

3. **Company Parameters:** *Describe your ideal customer's key parameters, including key metrics, behaviors, and brand characteristics.*

   Company parameters may include the number of employees, annual revenues, sales cycle lengths, or brand characteristics. After listing these parameters, prioritize them based on their relevance and importance. Clarify why you selected these parameters and the factors that influenced their ranking.

4. **Geographic Location:** *Determine where your ideal customer is located.*

   Even if you aspire to global success, start with a limited number of geographic locations to avoid spreading your marketing efforts too thin. Rank your top three locations and note why they are important.

As you work through each section, you may repeat points from your value proposition's target customer description or list the same traits in multiple

> *"Resist the temptation to include too many characteristics in your ICP. The goal is to narrow your focus, not to make it so broad that everyone fits."*

places. That's okay! Repetition will help highlight which qualities are core to your ICP and which are secondary. If certain sections aren't relevant to your business, just leave them blank.

A word of warning: Resist the temptation to include too many characteristics in your ICP. The goal is to narrow your focus, not to make it so broad that everyone fits. Capture its essence by summarizing your ideal customer in four to six bullet points.

Here are examples of ICPs for two companies mentioned earlier:

CampMap: a SaaS tool that helps campsites share details of their facilities with guests.

- Single-owner business

- Campsites with 200+ pitches

- Free and clear layout

- Premium/5-star positioning

- Caters to families with children

- Located in Croatia, Slovenia, Italy, or Germany

DOQSYS: a procurement advisory firm that helps enterprises transform their source-to-pay processes.

- Enterprises with 250 million EUR+ revenue and 10,000+ employees

- Purchasing function or department employs 5–10 professionals

- Locally centralized procurement process in place

- Local decision-making authority

- Tier 1/Tier 2 auto manufacturers

- Based in Hungary

If you're unsure about your ICP, create up to three and test your marketing strategies with each. Over time, you'll identify which one performs best. Keep in mind that scaling quickly may be difficult until you settle on a single ICP, as this ensures your client acquisition is highly focused. As your business evolves, your ICP may change, so it's important to revisit and refine it as needed.

Antavo's example illustrates this evolution: they started by targeting small businesses with their customer loyalty technology, then shifted their focus to mid-market clients, and ultimately identified enterprises as their ideal customer base. Reflecting on this journey, co-founder Zsuzsa Kecsmar remembers, "We started with specific industries like fashion and retail but evolved into an industry-agnostic loyalty solution, broadening our platform while staying true to its core strengths."

"You'll rely on three methods to acquire customers: outbound sales, partnerships, and inbound marketing."

The Launch Code: Pillar Two

"Structure your client acquisition" is the second pillar of *The Launch Code*, outlining three effective ways to reach and sell to your ideal customer. This pillar builds on the first one by providing actionable strategies to acquire clients and sets the stage for the third pillar, which focuses on scaling your operations.

You'll rely on three methods to acquire ideal customers: outbound sales, partnerships, and inbound marketing.

1. **Outbound Sales**: Proactively reaching out through calls, emails, or messages, targeting clients with personalized messages that present the benefits of your product or service.

2. **Partnerships**: Leveraging the reach and credibility of third-party organizations or businesses to acquire customers through collaboration.

3. **Inbound Marketing**: Creating valuable digital content, publicity, and events that attract prospects who actively seek solutions like yours.

While each of these methods serves a unique role in your client acquisition strategy, it's likely that one or two of them will have a greater impact on growing your customer base than others. Let's review each of these in further detail.

Module 4

Outbound Sales

* * *

O utbound sales involves proactively reaching out to potential clients, rather than waiting for them to show interest. It's the best way to acquire customers because you control the process and can quickly address obstacles in real-time. Direct contact with prospects gives you immediate feedback, which helps refine your offer and messaging. This, in turn, sharpens your value proposition, boosting the effectiveness of both

> *"Outbound sales is the best way to acquire customers because you control the process and can quickly address issues in real-time."*

your partnership and inbound marketing efforts.

Bence Marosi, co-founder of Dynamo Pricing, experienced the impact of doing outbound sales himself while pitching his dynamic ticket pricing tool to cinema chains. After reaching out to target clients in his local market, he realized there were not enough of them to sustain his business. He then expanded his outreach to include theaters, but discovered he could only engage with this market via the marketing platforms his target customers were already using.

"I realized I needed to target ticketing platforms," Bence recalls. "There are fewer platforms than end users—like theaters and sports teams—so I thought it was easier to sell to them first, then to their clients." Bence used this insight to overhaul his client acquisition strategy and sell to ticketing platforms worldwide.

Understand Your Sales Funnel

A key companion to your client acquisition strategy is the sales funnel—a visual representation of a prospect's journey from initial contact to final purchase. It's shaped like a funnel because prospects drop off at each stage, narrowing as leads move closer to becoming customers. While some follow the funnel step by step, others may drop out or move quickly from start to finish.

The sales funnel is equally crucial for tracking engagement through outbound sales, partnerships, and inbound marketing. It provides a systematic way

"Your sales funnel provides a systematic way to manage leads, improve conversion rates, and optimize your overall sales strategy."

to manage leads, improve conversion rates, and optimize your overall sales strategy by tailoring interactions to a prospect's stage, focusing on the most promising leads, and providing insights for revenue forecasting.

Dominik Mate Kovacs, founder of AI-based video generation startup Colossyan, describes his buyer's journey in an interview. "Customers discover our website and sign up for the product. They test it out, and share sample videos with their stakeholders, all without the need for credit card information. Periodically, they reach out to our sales team to inquire about upgrading to a more robust enterprise package. This approach has been instrumental in our growth," he explains.

A sales funnel has four main stages:

1. **Awareness**: *Prospects first learn about your product or service.*
    Introduce your offering and ensure prospects know it exists through outreach or awareness campaigns.

2. **Interest**: *Prospects engage with your content and explore how your product meets their needs.*
    Nurture leads by offering valuable information and building relationships through educational resources, webinars, and responding to inquiries.

3. **Consideration**: *Prospects evaluate your product against other options.*
    Convince people your solution is the best fit by organizing a discovery call or demo, addressing concerns, and creating proposals.

4. **Decision:** *Prospects are ready to decide.*
    Guide prospects to make an informed decision by negotiating terms, addressing objections, and closing the deal.

These stages can also be categorized as Top-of-Funnel (TOF), Middle-of-Funnel (MOF), and Bottom-of-Funnel (BOF). Regardless of the structure, communicate consistently, deliver value at every stage, and continuously refine your approach based on feedback.

Follow this Customer Acquisition Process

My Customer Acquisition Process (CAP) is a target account-based approach to implementing outbound sales. It covers identifying prospects and turning them into loyal customers. CAP isn't linear; it's a continuous loop where each cycle informs the next, driving continuous revenue growth. By following its six steps, you build a solid foundation for acquiring your first customers.

1. Determine Your Target Companies

Start by identifying 50–100 companies that fit your ideal customer profile (ICP). Research online using platforms like Google and LinkedIn, attend industry events, and tap your network to find these companies. Prioritize gathering a broad list of prospects and collect relevant information—news articles, profiles—into a CRM software like HubSpot, Pipedrive, or Salesforce, so you can refer to these later. This process will give you a solid prospect list to work from.

2. Identify Decision-Makers and Influencers

Next, identify decision-makers and influencers in these companies. Decision-makers have budget authority (e.g., CEOs or department heads), while influencers are subject matter experts who advise the decision-maker on purchases.

As Aleksander Niemczyk of Action Audit explains: "Typically, one key person makes the deal happen. It's usually a specialist with influence over the budget holder who sees the potential of our product and how it can be integrated into the company. When this person is in the organization, they usually become our customer."

In smaller companies, one person may handle all decisions, while larger companies may involve multiple stakeholders. Use LinkedIn, company websites, and industry events to identify people with relevant job titles like Head of IT or VP of Marketing and log them in your CRM.

"Identify a touchpoint—a shared connection or experience that builds trust with the buyer—early in the sales process and set the stage for engagement."

3. Find Your Touchpoint

Identify a touchpoint—a shared connection or experience that builds trust with the buyer—early in the sales process and set the stage for engagement.

The three most effective ones are:

- **Direct Contact**: A personal connection inside the target company.

- **Referral**: A shared friend, professional contact, or existing customer who can make an introduction.

- **Mutual Reference**: Someone you both know and can mention.

These touchpoints greatly improve your chances of a response since people are more likely to engage with someone they know, or someone connected via a trusted source. At first glance, this may seem identical to the "I know a guy" approach I dismissed earlier, yet there's one important difference: you focus on connecting to those who match your ICP, not simply reaching out to someone you happen to know. Using your network to connect with a decision-maker or influencer at a company matching your ICP is not just advisable, but preferred.

If no direct connections are available, look for shared interests, like a mutual alma mater, hometown, or hobby. For instance, I invited Joe De Sena, founder of endurance race company Spartan and bestselling author, as a guest on my *Launch Stories* podcast via email. The subject line: "Podcast invite from fellow Cornellian." He accepted right away.

4. Create a Top 10 Targets List

Narrow your list to ten high-priority targets. Managing dozens of conversations at once is impractical, so focusing on a smaller group will help prioritize your efforts.

Use these criteria to create your list:

- **Lead Warmth**: Companies with direct contacts, referrals, or mutual references.

- **Company Size**: Include a mix of small and large prospects, unless size is integral to your ICP.

- **Industry**: Target a single industry or approach multiple sectors to test which one works, unless your ICP is industry specific.

- **Geography**: Create a mix of local and international markets.

There's no single formula for creating your Top 10 list. Experiment with various approaches and expect it to evolve as you refine your value proposition. Keep your CRM updated and always ensure you have ten *active* prospects in your pipeline.

5. Initiate First Contact

Reach out to your Top 10 list to schedule a discovery call. Prioritize direct contacts, referrals, and mutual references. Mention your touchpoint in your email subject line or the first sentence of your message.

Your initial contact will lead to one of four outcomes:

- A meeting

- A referral to someone else in the company

- A rejection

- Silence

If your prospect wants to meet or refers you to someone else, follow up as needed. If they're not interested, thank them and ask them why not—is your solution not relevant or is now not a good time? If timing is an issue, make a note to reconnect later.

"The best way to manage a long sales cycle is to maintain a strong pipeline of prospects, so no single decision impacts your overall success."

If you get no response, follow up two or three more times using the messaging framework presented in Chapter 3. If there's still no reply, move on. You can either remove the company from your list or try reaching out later to a different contact.

6. Manage the Process to An Outcome

Guide the prospect through the sales funnel to a clear outcome. The ideal result is a "yes." A "no" is also acceptable, as it means you won't waste time on an uninterested prospect. The worst outcome is a "maybe," which leads to delays and wasted effort. Avoid these as much as possible. Whenever possible, clarify why a prospect isn't ready to decide now and set a follow-up date or deadline.

A typical B2B sales cycle can last up to a year, influenced by factors like product complexity, deal size, industry, stakeholder involvement, and approval processes. Sales and marketing alignment, competitive pressures, team efficiency, and customer relationships also play a role. The best way to manage a long sales cycle is to maintain a strong pipeline of prospects, so no single decision impacts your overall success.

Find the Right Touchpoint

Use these connections to create rapport with your target customer.

Direct Contact: Reach out directly, referencing a personal connection or recent interaction.

Referral: Ask a shared contact to introduce you.

Mutual Reference: Highlight someone you both know.

Birthplace/Nationality: Use shared origins, especially if you're abroad.

Place of Employment: Reference a shared workplace.

College/University: Mention a common alma mater, especially in US.

Member Organization: Cite involvement in the same professional group or club.

Hobby or Interest: Reference a shared hobby or sports team.

Conference/Event: Mention an event you both attended or spoke at.

Publication: Refer to a recent quote or article featuring them.

How to Boost Your Outbound Success

Mastering outbound sales takes time and practice. Regularly evaluate and adjust your approach to make it feel more natural. As you refine your process, you'll get better at identifying prospects, engaging confidently, and closing deals consistently.

Here are some tips to accelerate your success:

Write Your Own Referral: Make it easy for the referrer by drafting the introductory message yourself, so they just need to forward it. Ask them to cc you so you can follow up directly. Though some people may check with their contact before agreeing to provide an introduction, this approach is still more effective than cold outreach.

Follow Your Messaging Framework: Focus on the prospect's problem in all communications—emails, presentations, and conversations. Clearly demonstrate how your product or service solves their issue and stick to the messaging framework from Chapter 3. This will increase engagement and curiosity.

Reach the Decision-Maker: Always aim to speak directly with the decision-maker. While other conversations can provide useful insights, you gain control when you're talking to the person who can say "yes." Do everything you can to reach them.

Prepare to Handle Objections: After some time, you'll encounter the same objections, often around pricing, delivery, or reliability. Prepare to address them smoothly and use the feedback to refine your approach. Learn more about handling objections in Chapter 6.

Capture Deal Momentum: Watch for signs of growing momentum, such as a rapid exchange of calls and messages. When this happens, make your best and final offer to capitalize on the momentum and close the deal. Delaying could result in months of unproductive follow-up and lost opportunities.

* * *

Key Takeaways

- **Understand Your Sales Funnel**: A sales funnel helps visualize the journey prospects take from initial contact to final purchase. It enables you to tailor your approach at each stage (awareness, interest, consideration, decision) and optimize conversion rates.

- **Apply the Customer Acquisition Process (CAP)**: CAP is a continuous loop that guides outbound sales from identifying prospects to converting them into customers. Following this six-step framework helps refine outreach and establish a solid foundation for long-term growth.

- **Boost Outbound Success**: To accelerate outbound sales, focus on leveraging referrals, sticking to a consistent messaging framework, reaching decision-makers directly, handling objections, and capturing momentum to close sales efficiently.

Module 5

Partnerships

* * *

A partnership is a collaborative relationship between two businesses aimed at achieving shared goals. For early-stage businesses, partnerships are crucial for overcoming two major obstacles to acquiring new clients: a lack of credibility and limited resources. Startups often struggle to earn customer trust due to their lack of a proven track record and concerns about their long-term viability. A founder's personal or professional credibility can bridge this gap, but it may not be enough.

Additionally, startups often lack the resources—people, time, and money—for extensive sales and marketing activity, especially when expanding internationally. Founders can tackle these challenges by partnering with established companies or experienced individuals. These collaborations offer low-risk access to new customer bases and markets, helping to generate more revenue with less effort.

Types of Partnerships

Partnerships come in many forms and are referred to by different names depending on the nature of the relationship, industry, or geography. Common descriptions include affiliate, agent, broker, channel partner, dealer, distributor, intermediary, marketing partner, representative, reseller, value-added reseller, and wholesaler. Each one holds a unique place in a broader commercial strategy.

I've narrowed my focus to the three categories most relevant for startups: distributors, connectors, and agents.

Follow the Customer Acquisition Process detailed in Chapter 4 to identify, contact, and engage with these partners. You can either create separate processes for each type or use a single, unified process. Some targets may fit into multiple categories, so starting with one process is often more effective while you determine which form works best.

"Partnerships are crucial for overcoming two major obstacles to acquiring new clients: a lack of credibility and limited resources."

Let's explore how each type of partnership supports your client acquisition.

Distributor

A distributor is a partner that resells your product or service to end customers, often expanding your market reach through their established networks. Also known as resellers or wholesalers, distributors may offer a range of complementary products, boosting sales by combining your solution with others.

For instance, Antavo, a loyalty technology platform, partners with consultants who develop customer loyalty programs for major brands like Brewdog, Flying Tiger, and Notino. These consultants recommend

Antavo to support the implementation of their programs, helping the company access larger clients and fuel its international growth. Building and managing these relationships has become a critical element of the company's sales strategy.

Distributors may also buy products in bulk and resell them at a profit, as retailers like Tesco do with wholesale items. This model can drive significant sales, although often at lower margins.

Connector

A connector is a partner that consolidates similar customers and represents them to external entities, serving as a bridge between businesses and potential clients or collaborators. These organizations exist on local, national, and international levels across all industries, so the opportunity for building such partnerships is endless.

Connectors can be trade associations invested in the success of their industry members, such as the European Auto Manufacturers' Association, which can introduce its members to relevant service providers. This relationship benefits both parties: the connector supports its members, and the business gains access to a targeted client base.

Connectors can also be agencies that aggregate clients with similar needs and link them with suitable partners, a common practice in marketing services like ad buying.

Agent

An agent is a company or individual that represents your product or service to target customers, particularly in markets where you lack a direct presence. Unlike distributors, who focus on reselling products, agents work on your behalf during negotiations to protect your interests and secure favorable deals. They act as an extension of your internal sales team, offering localized expertise and connections.

For instance, D-TAG, a data intelligence platform, engaged a former pharmaceutical industry executive as an agent to broaden its reach in German-speaking countries and the UK. By leveraging this agent's insider knowledge and networks, the company was able to secure new business in this sector and expand into new markets without needing a full-time local team.

How to Build Win-Win Partnerships

The foundation of a successful partnership is a "win-win" approach, where both parties benefit equally and collaborate for mutual growth.

Two key elements must be in place for such an approach to work:

- **A Mutual Point of Interest**: Both parties should share a business connection, such as operating in the same industry, region, or targeting the same customer base. For example, if you sell a SaaS tool for warehouses, your ideal partner should already engage with warehouse clients or work within a similar sector. Partnerships that try to cover an excessively broad or unrelated market often lack focus and fail.

- **A Balanced Exchange of Benefits**: Each partner should gain advantages like financial growth, access to new markets, or enhanced credibility. A successful partnership offers equal value to both sides, ensuring long-term sustainability. If one party is consistently benefiting more than the other, the partnership is unlikely to endure. There is no such thing as a long-term one-sided relationship.

A well-structured partnership goes beyond simple transactions. It creates opportunities for both partners to leverage each other's strengths and evolves into a strategic relationship built on mutual trust and goodwill.

Follow these steps to build effective partnerships.

1. Define Your Ideal Partner

Identify the key traits you seek in a partner, just as you did while determining your Ideal Customer Profile (ICP). While no partner will be perfect, distinguish between essential traits and those that are "nice to have."

For example, I assisted Logiscool, a coding school for kids, in crafting a detailed profile for their ideal franchise partner that described the

"The foundation of a successful partnership is a 'win-win' approach, where both parties benefit equally and collaborate for mutual growth."

ideal mix of business experience, skills, personal traits, commitment level, and financial resources.

Logiscool first identified their ideal partner's motivation—franchisees aiming for profitability with a social impact. They detailed the desired franchisee's age, business experience, skills, and personal qualities. They stressed that franchisees should be owner-managers involved in daily operations and present on-site during the week. Financial requirements were also specified to cover the franchise fee, startup costs, and initial three to six months of operations.

This focused approach has helped Logiscool expand to 260 franchises in thirty-two countries.

2. Align Your Purpose

It's essential that you and your partner understand each other's purpose and ensure these are aligned. Otherwise, the collaboration can become ineffective, with each side rowing in opposite directions.

Begin by identifying the key benefits you seek, like increased sales or market access. Then, determine what you can offer your partner, such as new revenue streams, complementary products, or a competitive advantage. Finally, set measurable goals to achieve these mutual benefits.

3. Develop a Framework

Create a structure for your partnership that defines the nature of your collaboration.

Long-term partnerships involve ongoing arrangements, such as having a partner sell your products in a specific region or to a designated customer base. In contrast, short-term partnerships are often promotional and tied to a particular product or service for a set period. For example, I frequently collaborate with startup accelerators to promote *The Launch Code* group mentoring programs and workshops for a limited time.

Once the structure is defined, move on to negotiating the business model. This involves determining how costs, revenues, and profits will be allocated. It's crucial to apply the model to different scenarios and discuss the financial impacts for both parties. This process helps prevent potential disputes.

Avoid Exclusivity to Start

Just as you wouldn't rush into marriage with the first person you meet in a nightclub, avoid jumping into an exclusive business partnership too quickly. Treat the initial phase like dating: ensure that your business approaches, products, or services align, and that both parties are committed to a long-term relationship.

Some partners may demand exclusivity from the outset. Handle this request with care. You might inadvertently shoot yourself in the foot.

A European medical technology startup I advised signed an exclusive US distribution agreement that severely limited their international expansion options without any guaranteed revenue in return. They chose their partner based solely on bold promises and without any firsthand experience of working with the individual. By the time I became involved, it was evident that the partner had overpromised and would fail to deliver. Yet the founders were stuck in a poor deal that set back their growth for at least two years and had to resort to legal threats to exit the partnership.

Once you're sure the partnership is a good fit, you can consider exclusivity, but even then, it's smart to set clear boundaries on the product category, customer type, or region covered. Always negotiate for something in return, such as a minimum revenue guarantee or another financial benefit within a specified timeframe, otherwise you will find yourself in a lopsided relationship.

The best strategy is to maintain multiple, non-exclusive sales partnerships. This provides flexibility, reduces risks, and keeps your partners motivated to perform.

How to Manage a Partnership for Success

Negotiating a partnership is only the start; the real challenge lies in managing it effectively.

Even the best-planned partnerships can fail without proper oversight and execution. Proper

"The best strategy is to maintain multiple, non-exclusive sales partnerships."

management is especially critical when your product or service is just one among many in your partner's portfolio, and you want to be treated like a preferred partner.

Follow these guidelines to ensure your partnerships succeed.

Develop a Structured Onboarding Process: Provide your sales partner comprehensive training to ensure they understand your company's vision, strategy, and products. Give them access to essential sales materials—such as presentations, one-pagers, and videos—to help them communicate effectively with prospects and represent your brand accurately. Make sure they always have access to the latest materials.

Define Clear Success Metrics: Set clear, measurable goals such as revenue targets, lead conversions, or customer acquisitions, even if these are not listed as contractual obligations. By establishing specific targets and benchmarks, you can track the partnership's effectiveness and evaluate its impact on your business.

Assign Execution Responsibilities: Clearly define duties to avoid friction. While 80 percent of responsibilities are straightforward and well-defined, the remaining 20 percent often fall through the cracks. Assign these ambiguous tasks to one party to minimize misunderstandings, prevent poor execution, and ensure a smoother, more effective collaboration.

Establish Regular Checkpoints: Develop a schedule for regular check-ins—whether through written status reports or one-on-one meetings—to discuss performance, address challenges, and share insights. Frequent communication ensures accountability and keeps partners aligned with your evolving strategy.

Offer Your Partner Warm Leads: Though it might seem counterintuitive, pass along warm leads to your sales partner to demonstrate trust and strengthen the relationship. This will increase their motivation to invest in your product's success and enhance your importance within their portfolio. The opportunity to foster long-term collaboration often outweighs any short-term income loss from commissions.

Suggest Packaging Concepts: Consider bundling your product or service with elements from your partner's existing portfolio. By integrating your offering with their solutions, you can enhance the overall value proposition and boost the chances of a purchase. This creates a synergistic effect where the combined offering is greater than the sum of its parts.

Evaluate Long-Term Potential: Allow partners, particularly sales agents, a three-to-six-month window to demonstrate their capabilities. Don't make any long-term decisions about the business relationship before then. If they meet or exceed expectations, consider deepening their integration into your business as a long-term partner. Conversely, if performance falls short, assess whether a change is necessary.

* * *

Key Takeaways

- **Types of Partnerships**: Partnerships come in various forms, such as distributors, connectors, and agents, each playing a unique role in client acquisition. Distributors resell products, connectors bridge businesses with target customers, and agents represent products in new markets, offering localized expertise.

- **Building a Successful Partnership**: A successful partnership is built on shared goals and balanced benefits. Defining your ideal partner, aligning on purpose, and setting measurable goals ensure both parties benefit from the collaboration.

- **Managing a Partnership**: Effective partnership management requires structured onboarding, clear success metrics, and regular check-ins to ensure accountability. By offering support like warm leads and bundling products, you can strengthen the partnership and enhance long-term success.

Module 6

Inbound Marketing

* * *

Inbound marketing builds brand awareness and generates warm leads, guiding prospects through the sales funnel —from initial awareness to purchase. Unlike outbound sales or partnerships, which directly target specific prospects, inbound marketing allows customers to discover and engage with your business on their own. HubSpot reports that inbound leads are ten times more likely to convert into sales than outbound leads.

I've seen the impact of a strong inbound marketing presence firsthand. Often, a prospect who's followed my content online will reach out, and within twenty minutes of our first call, we close a deal, and they sign the contract the next day. This is when selling becomes more fun and less forced.

Ignoring content marketing means missing the opportunity to influence buyers early in the process. A McKinsey study shows that in an eleven-month B2B sales cycle, buyers contact sellers only in the eighth month after conducting 70 percent of their research independently. By the time they reach out, much of their decision-making has already occurred without direct sales interaction.

Inbound marketing requires consistent effort and patience. Sporadic LinkedIn posts aren't enough; you must regularly share valuable content aligned with your messaging across multiple platforms and actively engage in publicity and events for months. As your business scales, so does the impact of these efforts, making inbound marketing even more effective.

Key Forms of Inbound Marketing

Inbound marketing encompasses content marketing, social media, email marketing, pay-per click (PPC) advertising, display ads, search engine optimization (SEO), influencer and affiliate marketing, marketing automation, PR, and events. This variety can overwhelm founders new to sales and marketing.

> *"Ignoring content marketing means missing the opportunity to influence buyers early in the process."*

To keep it simple, I'll focus on the three inbound strategies most relevant for founder-led sales:

- **Digital Marketing**: Includes content creation, social media, email marketing, and online advertising.

- **Publicity**: Earned media coverage through news, features, or interviews from journalists or influencers.

- **Event Marketing**: Engaging at industry events, in person or online, to promote your company and connect with customers or partners.

The extent of your involvement in inbound marketing depends on your time and resources. As business grows, you can scale and increase your efforts accordingly.

Decide Your Content Elements

Effective inbound marketing starts with defining the topics that support your core message and attract customers, media, and event organizers.

Here's how to craft these content elements, step by step:

1. **Confirm Your Value Proposition**: Make sure your value proposition is valid as it's the foundation of your content strategy.

2. **Identify Proof Points**: Back up your value proposition with at least three facts, data points, or examples that prove your product's benefits and your credibility.

3. **Develop Content Themes**: Choose 3–5 topics that align with your value proposition and target audience's interests. These themes should educate and engage, not overtly sell. Your goal is to position yourself as an expert in your industry.

Create content on these topics for at least six months, consistently linking them to your brand to position yourself as an industry expert and build trust with customers, journalists, and event organizers.

Example: Creating Your Content Elements

Value Proposition

Enrol Consulting is an IT systems integrator that helps companies consolidate and simplify their business processes by integrating software tools into a single, easy-to-manage solution in just ten weeks.

Proof Points

- Twenty years of experience streamlining business processes

- Strong grasp of IT challenges for fast-growing businesses

- Introduced low-code tools at top companies like Lidl and Raiffeisen

Content Pillars

- Using low-code tools in IT project management

- Revealing the challenges of "Shadow IT"

- Data-driven application development

- Database integration and transformation

- IT challenges of high-growth businesses

Digital Marketing Building Blocks

Every online marketing project involves content, a call to action (CTA), distribution, and promotion. These components can be combined into a single social media post or a comprehensive multi-platform campaign.

Start by testing a simple initiative. As you gain experience and confidence, you can integrate multiple projects into a unified strategy.

> *"Every online marketing project involves content, a call to action, distribution, and promotion."*

1. **Content**: Fuel your marketing

Examples: *blog article, case study, checklist, course, ebook, infographic, podcast, poll, post, presentation, quiz, quote, survey, testimonial, video, webinar, whitepaper, worksheet.*

Fresh, valuable content attracts attention, builds interest, and encourages engagement. Each piece you create should serve one of three goals:

- **Attract (Top-of-Funnel)**: Build visibility and engagement by showcasing yourself or your organization. Tell motivational stories and use humor to inspire your audience and highlight your values and beliefs.

- **Nurture (Middle-of-Funnel)**: Showcase your expertise and build rapport with your audience. Share mistakes, myths, successes, comparisons, tips, insights, and tools to help your customers improve results and spark virtual conversations.

- **Convert (Bottom-of-Funnel)**: Promote your offering to your audience. Include content with social proof, benefits of your product, and special offers that turn prospects into customers.

Be careful to consistently publish content that balances all three objectives—*attract, nurture, and convert.* Relying solely on TOF content may boost brand recognition but won't establish your expertise or clarify what you're selling. Focusing only on MOF content can showcase your expertise but might fail to build personal connections or communicate what's available for purchase. Producing only BOF content risks making you seem overly sales-focused. Aim for a balanced content mix across all platforms: 40 percent "Attract," 40 percent "Nurture," and 20 percent "Convert."

For example, German biotech company Computomics uses a multi-channel content strategy to showcase its agricultural expertise and humanize its brand. They share blogs, host podcasts, and organize webinars on plant breeding innovations and machine learning's impact on the food industry. On LinkedIn, they promote this content alongside updates on industry events, customer collaborations, awards, and team activities like their annual BBQ and bike-to-work initiative.

Remember to repurpose content across formats—for example, turning a blog post into an infographic or a social media update. Use a content calendar to plan your content in advance and maintain a steady, balanced mix across platforms. As Radek Novotny from Superface.ai says, "I really love this approach—it gives me a way to build content in a repeatable way, with a plan for tomorrow, the next day, and beyond."

2. **Call to Action**: Encourage prospects to engage

Examples: *book now, download, fill out, get started, learn more, meet with us, order, preview, register, request a demo, schedule, sign up, start free trial, subscribe, try now*

Prompt your audience to act by including CTAs in your content. It's a great way to measure the effectiveness of specific campaigns.

CTAs fall into three categories:

- **Access Content**: Offer free resources like guides or case studies in exchange for email addresses.

- **Schedule Meetings**: Encourage prospects to book a discovery call.

- **Drive Purchase**: Guide them to buy your product or register for your service.

There's no need to include a CTA in every piece of content but incorporate them regularly so you can experiment with different ones and see which ones work best.

3. **Distribution**: Reach prospects where they are

Examples: *blog site, email, landing page, newsletter, podcast, social media, website, webinar*

Distribute your content across multiple platforms to reach prospects in different contexts. Most potential customers lurk for months before engaging with you: they will follow your LinkedIn posts, visit your website, and subscribe to your newsletter.

I realized this when a prospect once began a discovery call with me by saying he already "knew me well." While I tried to recall if we had met before, he explained that he had been following my LinkedIn posts and reading my newsletter for the past year, which made him feel as though he knew me personally.

It's a good idea to have three distribution channels in place:

- **Website/Landing Page**: Your digital home base for directing leads to download, sign up, or purchase. Whether it's your main website or a dedicated landing page, ensure it aligns with your marketing style and emphasizes a single CTA.

- **Social media**: Platforms like LinkedIn (crucial for B2B sales), YouTube, Facebook, Instagram, Twitter, and TikTok offer broad reach for promoting content. Host detailed content on your website and link to it from social posts. For example, share a blog summary on LinkedIn with a link to the full post and a CTA.

- **Email Newsletter**: Use lead magnets or webinars to build an email list for nurturing prospects who need more time. Send targeted follow-ups and create a recurring newsletter with insights or product updates. Tools like Mailchimp, HubSpot, or ActiveCampaign can streamline and automate your efforts.

4. **Promotion**: Amplify your impact

Use unpaid and paid methods to boost awareness of your content and achieve a greater impact.

- **Links/Co-Marketing**: Share links to your content via social media or email, or partner with organizations that already reach your target audience. Co-marketing agreements allow them to distribute your content through their channels, helping you to tap into their credibility and audience.

- **Digital Advertising**: Use pay-per-click (PPC) ads to drive traffic to your landing page. These can include display ads, social media ads, search ads, or remarketing ads targeting previous site visitors. While not always essential, PPC can be a worthwhile investment when boosting reach increases your return on investment.

Example: Creating Digital Marketing Initiatives

I applied the four building blocks of inbound marketing across different projects, using the same product—how to create a value proposition—but varying the content and promotion strategies. By adapting content, CTAs, distribution, and promotion, I tailored each campaign to achieve specific goals.

Here's how I crafted these content pillars:

1. **Scenario**: *Free Access, Free Distribution*
   - **Goal**: Build brand awareness and engagement at no cost
   - **Content**: Free blog article
   - **Call to Action**: Read Article
   - **Distribution**: Website
   - **Promotion**: Social media posts, email

2. **Scenario**: *Free Access, Paid Distribution*
   - **Goal**: Positioned service, present a promotional offer, and expand my audience
   - **Content**: Live webinar
   - **Call to Action**: Sign Up
   - **Distribution**: Landing Page, delivery via group video
   - **Promotion**: Social media posts, email, PPC ads

3. **Scenario**: *Paid Access, Paid Distribution*
   - **Goal**: Prioritized revenue generation over brand awareness
   - **Content**: Video course
   - **Call to Action**: Click to Buy
   - **Distribution**: Landing Page, delivery via education platform
   - **Promotion**: Social media posts, email, PPC ads

Get Free Exposure Through Publicity

Add a second layer to your inbound marketing by targeting media outlets aligned with your content themes. Choose platforms that appeal to your target audience, whether customers or business partners, and focus on relevant industries or topics.

Online Platforms: Leverage webinars, articles, blogs, and podcasts specific to your industry. Explore opportunities across multiple online channels to broaden your reach.

Offline Media: Traditional outlets like TV, radio, newspapers, and magazines can significantly boost credibility and authority. For instance, appearing on TV news or entrepreneurial shows like *Shark Tank* or *Dragon's Den* provides unmatched exposure.

Guest Writing: Contribute guest articles in industry blogs or print media to build authority. Offer valuable insights and include examples or case studies from your business to connect with readers.

Using a mix of media channels helps amplify your message and establish your brand across various audiences.

Using Events to Build Exposure

While digital strategies are vital, live events are equally important. They offer unique opportunities to boost your profile, grow your network, and build awareness. I find that face-to-face interactions with industry professionals and potential clients can leave lasting impressions that digital channels often cannot match.

Here are five ways to leverage events, ranked from lowest to highest impact:

Attendee: Attending is the simplest way to benefit. Use the opportunity to network, generate leads, and start relationships with attendees and speakers that can be nurtured over time.

For instance, Bence at Dynamo Pricing implemented his revised outbound sales strategy by attending a ticketing conference in Birmingham, where he connected with a dozen ticketing platforms across the UK, Europe, and North America. This

"Events offer unique opportunities to boost your profile, grow your network, and build awareness."

resulted in partnerships with Spectrix, the UK's largest ticketing provider, and Tickets.com in the US.

Exhibitor: Renting a booth lets you showcase your product or service, offering more visibility than attendance alone. While it comes with a cost, you can maximize your return by scheduling advance meetings with key prospects in addition to relying on foot traffic.

Panelist: Participating in a panel positions you as an expert. Panels discuss industry topics, and your insights can boost credibility and align you with respected professionals with whom you share the stage. Reach out to event organizers and offer your expertise on specific topics where you can provide value to secure a panelist spot. Over time, as your reputation grows, invitations to join panels may come to you without the need to pitch.

Speaker: Delivering a presentation establishes you as a thought leader. Focus on delivering value to the audience, not just promoting your business. Start by pitching yourself to event organizers, but as your personal brand expands, speaking invitations may follow.

Fireside Chat Guest: Being interviewed by an industry expert on stage cements your authority. This relaxed, informal format is ideal for sharing key messages and leaving a strong impression. By the time you reach this level, you should have significant accomplishments that make your perspective valuable to others.

If you want to contribute to an event, review its website to identify key topics that align with your expertise and themes. Then, seek a referral or directly contact the agenda coordinator to explore opportunities. They may direct you to submit a proposal via an online form, leaving it to them to follow up if interested.

Pick Your Spots

Inbound marketing is essential for growing your business and generating warm leads, but it can be daunting. Rather than doing too much at once, focus on a few activities that fit your product, skills, comfort zone, and budget. Experiment with various content types and distribution channels and pitch yourself, for example, as a guest on industry podcasts. Complement digital efforts with in-person events to connect with prospects and boost your profile through speaking opportunities. As you learn what works, you can confidently expand your efforts as your team and resources grow.

* * *

Key Takeaways

- **Drive Engagement Through Inbound Marketing**: Inbound marketing encompasses content marketing, social media marketing, and SEO, enabling potential customers to find and engage with your brand on their own. This method nurtures leads through the sales funnel, with inbound leads being more likely to convert than outbound leads.

- **Build Impact with Digital Marketing Essentials**: Successful online marketing hinges on four essential elements: content, call to action, distribution, and promotion. A well-balanced strategy that uses these components across multiple channels ensures consistent engagement and guides prospects through each stage of the buying journey.

- **Boost Visibility Through Publicity and Events**: Publicity through media outlets like news articles, podcasts, and TV appearances enhances brand credibility. Attending, exhibiting at, or speaking at events offers valuable networking opportunities and significantly boosts brand visibility and authority.

Craft Your Winning Sales Recipe

* * *

In this chapter, I've shared the three key pathways to client acquisition: outbound sales, partnerships, and inbound marketing. Together, they form the foundation of a sales strategy designed to connect you with your ideal customer.

While it would be convenient if a universal formula for success existed, the reality is that every founder must experiment, adjust, and refine their approach to find the mix that helps them close more deals with less effort. Crafting this sales recipe requires identifying which strategies resonate most with your audience.

Even within a single sales strategy, the effectiveness of specific tactics will vary:

- In outbound sales, LinkedIn outreach might yield higher response rates than email campaigns.

- In partnerships, independent agents may bring in more qualified leads than large-scale distributors.

- In inbound marketing, participating in industry events might outperform publishing blog posts in generating immediate client interest.

Finding the right mix isn't about luck—it's about patience and persistence. Through testing and iteration, you'll uncover the strategies that align with your business goals and drive consistent revenue. While this process of trial and error may feel slow, it's essential for building a scalable, predictable sales engine.

In sales, as in cooking, the recipe for success isn't about following a fixed formula—it's about finding the right ingredients for your unique taste.

> *"Finding the right mix isn't about luck—it's about patience and persistence."*

Eureka! 160 Percent Revenue Growth!

The sales journey of Eureka Consulting & Games highlights the power of a structured approach to client acquisition.

Co-founders Peter Kalmar and Gabriella Bodi launched the organizational development firm in 2014, driven by a desire to create positive work environments through team-building games. They later added leadership consulting and training services.

Initially, they relied on personal connections, cold outreach, and Google (search and ads) to secure clients. While this worked in a market with few alternatives, competition increased, and their lead quality and growth declined. "The quality and quantity of our leads declined, and we realized that generating leads purely through our website would not sustain the business," Peter explains. COVID-19 temporarily boosted demand for their online services, but this advantage faded as the pandemic eased.

Faced with these challenges, Peter and Gabriella decided to implement *The Launch Code*. They sharpened Eureka's value proposition and began addressing their prospects' key problems in their outreach instead of overwhelming them with a list of services. They transitioned from a scattergun approach to focusing on their ICP: human resources managers at companies with 50–100 employees that had recently reorganized their teams.

Peter applied the Customer Acquisition Process to target business hotels and conference centers, successfully securing reseller agreements with 10 percent of the 200 he contacted. He offered conference organizers gamified experiences, delivered keynotes, and attended their events. In parallel, Eureka strengthened its inbound marketing through LinkedIn posts, newsletters, and webinars, attracting a highly targeted audience.

These three-pronged efforts led to extraordinary results: Eureka's revenue skyrocketed by 160 percent in 2023, with an additional 75 percent growth projected for the following year. Their lead conversion rate reached 40 percent, and they secured a three-year strategic relationship with a major automobile brand.

This structured approach gave Eureka's founders the results they had longed for. "We used to spend most of our time on operational tasks and dreamed of smoother processes and predictable revenue," Peter recalls. "Now we have more clients, higher income, a larger team, and time for our personal lives."

THE LAUNCH CODE™

FOCUS

YOUR OFFER
AND MESSAGE,
SO PROSPECTS
UNDERSTAND WHAT
YOU'RE SELLING

VALUE PROPOSITION

PRODUCT OFFERING

MESSAGING & TOOLS

STRUCTURE

YOUR CLIENT
ACQUISITION,
SO YOU CLOSE MORE
DEALS WITH
LESS EFFORT

OUTBOUND SALES

PARTNERSHIPS

INBOUND MARKETING

SCALE

YOUR OPERATIONS,
SO YOU SUSTAIN
LONG-TERM GROWTH
AND EMPOWER
YOUR TEAM.

GOAL SETTING

PERFORMANCE TRACKING

TEAM DEVELOPMENT

CHAPTER 5

Scale Your Operations

"You're only a startup once. You don't need to be a startup
forever. You need to get to the next stage."
— *Brian Chesky (co-founder of Airbnb)*

Andrei Danescu commands attention from the moment you meet him. With a background as a Formula One racing systems engineer, he comes across as serious and focused. When he begins discussing his robotics and data intelligence startup, Dexory, Andrei's energy shifts; his enthusiasm becomes infectious. This passion, combined with a relentless drive, is what has propelled the UK startup to become a leader in warehouse logistics.

Andrei's co-founder, Oana Jinga, offers a composed counterbalance to his high-energy approach. Drawing from years of sales and business development experience at Google and Telefonica, her steady demeanor complements Andrei's intensity. Together, they make a formidable team—one that also happens to be a husband-and-wife duo.

Dexory is transforming warehouse operations with cutting-edge technology. The company's flagship innovation, an autonomous robot capable of scanning a 10,000-square-meter warehouse in a few hours, provides real-time visibility into inventory. This solution optimizes space, improves stock management, and empowers logistics providers to operate more efficiently.

When I began working with Andrei and Oana in early 2021, Dexory had just eight employees and a few hundred thousand pounds in revenue. They were in the middle of transitioning from serving retail customers to focusing on the logistics sector and needed help refining their sales strategy. We applied *The Launch Code* to sharpen their value proposition and developed a go-to-market strategy tailored to their new target audience.

Since then, Dexory's growth has been extraordinary. By late 2024, the company had scaled to 160 employees, projected $10 million in annual recurring revenue, and raised $120 million across three funding rounds. This rapid ascent underscores the strength of their product and the clarity of their sales strategy.

What fueled this remarkable transformation?

Andrei and Oana recognized the importance of scaling their operations to meet the growing demands of their business.

From Chaos to Clarity

Scaling was easier said than done. As Dexory closed more deals and grew its team, the need for clearer structure and processes became apparent. Without aligned goals, employees struggled to prioritize effectively, and progress stalled. Operating without a system to track results meant they couldn't measure what worked.

Organizational change proved equally challenging. Some early employees couldn't adapt to the demands of a larger team, and some new hires underperformed. Their first senior sales leader, despite a strong resume, left after five months. He struggled to meet the demands of a fast-paced startup environment, expecting to operate in a predefined structure rather than actively helping to shape and build it.

To address these hurdles, Andrei and I worked on introducing operational principles to support rapid delivery while fostering accountability. These measures allowed him to step back from daily operations, empowering his team while focusing on innovation and investor relations.

By implementing a goal-setting framework, Dexory aligned company objectives with individual contributions. Initially, their ambitious goals overwhelmed the team, but after refining their approach, they established quarterly targets and held regular road-mapping and progress meetings. This created accountability without burdening the team with unnecessary bureaucracy.

Andrei reflects on this learning curve. "You don't want to make targets overly complex or the reporting process too onerous, but you can't ignore them either. Scaling a business is about balance. If you hire great people, you can delegate. If not, and let go anyway, you're going to get burned. You need to be strategic, or your company culture can suffer."

Dexory's sales operations have flourished under a new sales leader who introduced essential structure and streamlined processes, complemented by the strategic insights of an experienced marketing head. This strengthened leadership enabled Andrei and Oana to redefine their roles in sales—empowering their team to operate independently while maintaining visibility of key accounts.

"We don't want to be on every sales call," Oana explains. "But we need to stay aware of account progress and address obstacles as they arise."

Dexory has transformed from a struggling startup into a leader in its field. By restructuring their operations, introducing operating guidelines, and building their team, Andrei and Oana have positioned the company for long-term success. Their journey is a testament to the importance of scaling operations, so you, as a founder, can focus on strategy and growth.

What Got You Here, Won't Get You There

In earlier chapters, we explored how to lay the groundwork for effective selling—starting with developing a focused offer and message, followed by implementing a structured client acquisition strategy. While these principles help secure initial deals, achieving predictable and growing revenue demands a systematic approach to execution, as well.

Don't get me wrong. Some chaos is both normal and inevitable in the early stages of building a business. After all, startups are about creating "something from nothing." During this phase, founders often rely on gut instincts and wear many hats, navigating an evolving identity and operations. But over time, this freewheeling approach stops being inspiring. Instead, it leads to exhaustion, inefficiency, and team-wide confusion—obstacles that stall sustainable growth.

Founders can overcome this challenge by shifting their mindset from *building* a business to *operating* one. This transition can feel uncomfortable. Many founders resist this change, especially those without experience working in well-structured, often corporate environments. Even those who attempt it often underestimate what it entails.

> *"Founders can overcome this challenge by shifting their mindset from building a business to operating one."*

Navigating this transformation successfully involves embracing three fundamental truths.

- **Recognize the Limits of Early Methods**: The tactics that got you from "zero to one" won't take you from "one to one hundred." It's not a matter of better or worse—it's just different.

- **Structure Enables Innovation**: Contrary to what many founders fear, introducing structure does not stifle creativity. It does the opposite. Having processes in place frees up time and mental bandwidth for testing and refining ideas. Without them, you risk wasting energy reinventing the wheel on a daily basis.

- **Find the Right Balance**: There's no need to swing from complete chaos to rigid over-structuring. Overly bureaucratic environments, like the one I experienced at NBCUniversal, can smother innovation. On the other hand, entrepreneurial settings, even at large companies like SBS Broadcasting, show that clear expectations paired with operational freedom drive success. Your goal should be to gradually implement enough structure to support efficient growth while retaining the flexibility to adapt.

151

While my focus is on sales and marketing, this approach applies across your organization. Setting clear goals, tracking performance metrics, and defining roles are just as vital in product development, finance, and customer service.

Founders who embrace this approach unlock the ability to scale effectively. By creating clarity across their organization, they can focus on making strategic decisions that ensure long-term growth.

The Launch Code: Pillar Three

"Scale your operations" is the third pillar of *The Launch Code*, highlighting three critical elements for effective execution: goal setting, performance tracking, and team development. This builds on the second pillar by ensuring the foundations for scaling are in place as your business expands.

You'll focus on three areas to scale operations effectively:

1. **Goal Setting**: Defining clear, actionable objectives for your organization ensures alignment and keeps everyone focused on priorities that drive meaningful progress. Break goals into manageable steps to maintain momentum and clarity across teams.

2. **Performance Tracking**: Regularly measuring outcomes against defined metrics enables you to make informed, data-driven decisions. This approach eliminates reliance on gut feelings and fosters accountability throughout the organization.

3. **Team Development**: Building your team around defined roles and responsibilities allows you to hire strategically.

Empowering individuals with clarity and ownership fosters high performance and enhances operational efficiency.

Mastering these three areas ensures your business has the structure in place to grow sustainably. Let's explore each element in detail.

Goal Setting

* * *

I've long understood the value of goal setting and made planning—identifying the steps and resources needed to reach my goals—central to my personal and professional growth. Many founders, however, see things differently. Some dismiss planning as a waste of time, with one even telling me, "If you're planning, you're not doing."

While planning may feel unnecessary, it's crucial for scaling a business. Without clear objectives, you can't measure progress, prioritize efforts, or avoid getting bogged down in day-to-day

> *"Pause occasionally and ask, 'what do I want to achieve with my business, and how will I get there?'"*

operations. The solution? Pause occasionally and ask, "What do I want to achieve with my business, and how will I get there?"

Answering these questions offers immediate benefits: a clear vision of success, easier progress tracking, the ability to identify obstacles and adjust actions, and a stronger ability to say "no" to distractions. With a clear destination, you'll also stay resilient in the face of setbacks, making challenges feel worthwhile.

That said, I don't advocate for the exhaustive planning typical of large corporations, where endless analysis delays action. Instead, adopt a light-touch approach: every few months, spend a few hours reflecting on goals, evaluating strategies, and identifying your best options. Write down your plan and commit to testing it.

Your plan should fit on two pages and, at most, a single spreadsheet. I call it a *Simple Plan*—just enough structure to guide early-stage businesses toward sustainable growth.

Get the Most from Your Simple Plan

A *Simple Plan* is built around four components: focus areas, goals, key performance indicators (KPIs), and actions. To ensure its effectiveness, your plan should meet these essential criteria:

- **Clear Direction**: Your plan outlines the outcome you want and breaks it into actionable steps with milestones to track your progress.

- **Specific but Adaptable**: While your goals are defined, the methods to achieve them remain flexible. As you execute your plan, use feedback to refine and update it based on what's working and what isn't.

- **Measurable**: Incorporate numbers, percentages, or deadlines to make progress evaluation objective and straightforward. Test it by asking: "In the future, can I clearly tell if I achieved this goal?"

- **Written Down**: Documenting your plan forces clarity, creates a reference point, and strengthens your commitment. Without a written plan, it's easy to forget, misinterpret, or abandon your goals entirely.

Studies consistently show the benefits of written goals and actionable plans. For example, a widely cited study conducted with the graduating classes of Harvard Business School in 1953 and 1979 revealed:

- 84 percent had not set any goals.

- 13 percent had written goals but no concrete plan.

- 3 percent had both written goals and a clear plan.

Ten years later, the results were remarkable:

- The 13 percent with written goals were earning twice as much as the 84 percent without goals.

- The 3 percent with both goals and plans were earning *ten times* more than the other 97 percent combined.

While the study's authenticity has been questioned, its conclusion aligns with my personal experience: identifying your goals and planning the steps to achieve them is crucial for success.

The real challenge? Striking the right balance: *how* to plan effectively without overloading yourself or your team. Keep it simple, clear, and actionable to build a roadmap that drives results.

Follow This Simple Plan Process

My five-step planning process helps you create a Simple Plan in two hours or less.

Start by choosing your planning period. If you're in the early stages or new to planning, begin with a three-month plan. As your business stabilizes, you can extend it to six months and eventually transition to an annual plan.

Planning for less than three months won't allow enough time to assess progress, while planning beyond a year will shift your focus to long-term vision instead of immediate priorities. We'll cover how to create your long-term vision in Chapter 7.

Let's go through each planning step one by one.

1. Identify Your Focus Areas

Start by identifying your business's key focus areas. For most founders, these typically fall into four categories:

- **Product or Service** (e.g., offerings and features)
- **Sales and Marketing** (e.g., outbound efforts, partnerships, inbound strategies)
- **Organization** (e.g., team development, operational efficiency)
- **Other** (e.g., fundraising, brand building, industry recognition)

For each category, consider what you want to achieve during the planning period. You might prioritize developing more product features, improving outbound sales efforts, or hiring more salespeople. You may also set a focal point outside these core areas, like raising venture capital funding.

Summarize each focus area in three or four words, such as:

- **Product**: Increase product functionality
- **Sales and Marketing**: Boost customer outreach

157

- **Organization**: Expand sales team

- **Other**: Raise VC funding

Make these descriptions clear enough to guide your direction but avoid precise details or metrics for now. You'll define those later. Keep in mind that as your business evolves, your focus areas will change. What you prioritize today may become routine in the future, so expect shifts in focus from one planning period to the next.

> *"Keep in mind that as your business evolves, your focus areas will change."*

2. Assign Owners and Stakeholders

Assign a responsible person within your team to own each focus area and ensure it remains a priority. Depending on your stage, you or your co-founders may oversee multiple areas. Avoid multiple owners for one focus area to prevent confusion and miscommunication. While the owner is accountable for success, they should identify stakeholders—co-founders, team members, or external partners—who will support them. The owner's role is to ensure stakeholders contribute to achieving the goals.

3. Set Your Financial Targets

Setting financial targets is crucial for managing your business, as the language of business is numbers. A *Simple Plan* focuses on four key financial areas: revenues, costs, net income, and profit margin. The level of detail depends on your company's stage and your financial expertise. Start simple and add complexity as your business grows.

Familiarity with spreadsheet tools like Excel will make preparing your financial plan easier. If you're not comfortable with spreadsheets, consider taking a course or delegating the task to someone who can create simple templates for you.

There are two primary approaches to financial planning: top-down and bottom-up.

Top-down planning involves analyzing market trends and competitors to estimate total spending in your niche and predict your market share. For example, if you aim to capture 1 percent of a €500 million market, your revenue target would be €5 million. This approach works well for established companies in mature markets but may be less relevant for early-stage startups creating new markets.

Bottom-up planning is more detailed and estimates revenue based on expected product sales. For example, if your product costs €10,000 and you plan to sell to twenty-five customers, your revenue target would be €250,000.

Distinguish between one-time revenues from project-based work and recurring revenues from subscription models. If possible, categorize revenues by product type, customer type, or region, and break these down by month. Use bottom-up planning to estimate your monthly costs for categories like office rent, salaries, and marketing.

These revenue and cost estimates will help project net income and profit margin. Net income is the total profit (or loss) after subtracting all expenses from revenue, while profit margin shows the percentage of revenue that remains as profit after costs, indicating how efficiently your company converts revenue into profit.

If applicable, use past performance as a reference to set future targets, ensuring growth instead of stagnation or decline. Include columns in your spreadsheet comparing your plan to the same period from the previous year. This allows you to assess which parts of your business are growing or shrinking.

4. Determine Your Goals and KPIs

With your focus areas and financial targets set, the next step is to define your goals and key performance indicators (KPIs) for the planning period. Though often used interchangeably, a goal is the specific outcome you aim to achieve, while a KPI tracks your progress toward that outcome.

For example:

- Your goal could be to increase monthly recurring revenue to €50,000.

- A related KPI might be the number of new subscriptions acquired each month.

As Matteo Berlucchi of Healthily reminds us, identifying what success looks like is critical to scaling your organization. "You need a very clear set of objectives and key results, to make it clear to everyone what they're supposed to do. You create this cascade of objectives, starting with the top one, and from there you can drive all the other things."

For each focus area, set a maximum of one to three goals to avoid overwhelm and ensure you remain focused on what matters most. Make sure each goal is realistic, aligned with your long-term objectives, and achievable with your current resources, assuming no major disruptions.

Next, assign one to three KPIs to each goal, especially if the goal is difficult to measure. For instance, if your goal is to close €1 million in new business by year-end, your KPIs could include contacting twenty-five new prospects by March 30, closing three new clients in the pharmaceutical sector, and raising your average

"For each focus area, set a maximum of one to three goals to avoid overwhelm and ensure you remain focused on what matters most."

contract value to €75,000. Collectively, these KPIs will help you reach your overall goal.

Goals like improving employee satisfaction or ensuring product quality are harder to quantify and may require subjective assessments. In these cases, use your gut feeling to evaluate where you stand on a scale of one to ten, where "one" means you're just starting, and "ten" means you've fully achieved the goal with no room for improvement. This initial assessment becomes your KPI. When you review your progress, reassess using the same scale to gauge how close you are to achieving your goal. While this approach may not be as concrete as revenue targets, my experience with founders shows that if you're honest with yourself, your internal compass can reliably indicate your progress.

In addition to goal-specific KPIs, it's valuable to track other metrics that assess your overall business performance, known as Operational KPIs. These provide insight into efficiency and highlight areas for improvement. The most common KPIs are listed in the sidebar.

Not all operational KPIs will be relevant to your business. Focus on the most important ones to avoid information overload. It's better to consistently track three to five key KPIs than to spread yourself thin by monitoring too many, which can dilute your focus.

Top Sales & Marketing KPIs

Sales KPIs

1. **Monthly Recurring Revenue (MRR)**: The revenue generated monthly, calculated by multiplying the average revenue per user (ARPU) by the number of active users or customers.

2. **Revenue Growth Rate**: The percentage increase in revenue over a specific period, calculated by comparing the revenue from the current and previous periods.

3. **Average Revenue Per User (ARPU)**: The average revenue generated from each active customer, calculated by dividing MRR by the total number of active users.

4. **Average Contract Value (ACV)**: The average value of a customer contract over its duration.

5. **Customer Lifetime Value (LTV)**: The total revenue a customer is expected to generate during their relationship with your business.

6. **Lead Conversion Rate**: The percentage of leads that convert into paying customers, indicating sales effectiveness and product demand.

7. **Customer Renewal Rate**: The percentage of customers who renew their contracts or subscriptions over a given period.

Marketing KPIs

1. **Customer Acquisition Cost (CAC)**: The cost of acquiring a new customer, calculated by dividing total acquisition expenses by the number of new customers.

2. **Qualified Leads**: The number of leads that meet specific criteria, focusing on quality over quantity to assess the success of your marketing efforts.

3. **Website Visitors/Traffic**: Tracks the number of inbound visitors to your website, reflecting brand awareness and outreach efforts.

4. **Advertising Effectiveness**: Measures the number of leads generated and the conversion rate from advertising campaigns.

5. **Social Media Engagement**: Tracks how well your content resonates with the audience through likes, shares, and comments, helping expand brand reach.

5. Develop an Action Plan

To finish your planning, create an action plan that breaks each goal into specific actions, providing clear steps for execution. Organize the plan by focus areas, listing your goals under each, and then detail the actions required to achieve those goals, setting deadlines for each. It's important to distinguish between goals and actions: a goal is the desired outcome, while an action is a step taken toward achieving that outcome. This will guide your implementation and establish milestones to keep you on track throughout the planning period.

The number of action items for each goal depends on your preference, but avoid excessive detail. Instead, prioritize the most impactful steps by applying the Pareto Principle (80/20 Rule)—focus Mon the 20 percent of actions that will yield 80 percent of the results. This keeps your action plan effective and manageable.

To go further, consider using a spreadsheet or project management tool to create a Gantt Chart, a visual planning tool that outlines a project schedule. It displays tasks or activities along a timeline, showing when each task begins and ends, as well as their duration. Gantt charts help visualize the timeline for each action, preventing over-scheduling and ensuring a balanced plan, while providing a clear overview to help ensure tasks are completed on schedule.

Align Your Planning Elements

As you finalize your *Simple Plan*, ensure that your focus areas, financial targets, goals, KPIs, and actions are aligned. This creates a clear link between your long-term objectives and day-to-day operations.

For example, if you set a revenue target of €100,000, your goals and KPIs should reflect enough clients (e.g., twenty) and revenue per client (e.g., €5,000) to meet that target. Also, ensure you have the necessary resources to achieve your goals. If one of your goals is to build an email list of 10,000 subscribers, make sure your marketing budget accounts for the costs of acquiring those subscribers.

As your business matures, you'll break down company goals and KPIs into smaller objectives for each department, team, or individual. This level of detail ensures that every team member understands their role in the company's success and how their performance will be measured.

Ákos Gergely of DOQSYS experienced firsthand the transformative impact of applying this planning approach to his business. He collaborated with his sales manager to create an annual plan divided into quarterly goals and actionable steps. This aligned his team's focus and clarified priorities. Using the *Simple Plan* template, Ákos produced a concise, well-balanced document that effectively tracks progress without overwhelming detail.

"This approach to planning gave us clarity and direction," he explains. "Now we have a focused plan that is not too long, not too detailed, and it keeps everyone aligned and motivated, helping us stay on track and achieve our goals."

Sample Focus, Goals, and KPIs

1. Focus/Product or Service: Increase product functionality

Goal: Launch version 2.0 of software platform by December 1st

KPIs:

- Percentage of development milestones completed on time
- Number of successful beta tests conducted prior to launch
- Customer satisfaction score from beta users

—

2. Focus/Sales and Marketing: Boost customer outreach

Goal: Contact 100 customers and close ten deals worth 200K EUR each by year-end

KPIs:

- Number of customer outreach attempts made per week
- Conversion rate of contacted customers to closed deals
- Total revenue generated from closed deals

3. Focus/Organization: Expand sales team

Goal: Hire a sales director with a tech commercial background by March 1st

KPIs:

- Number of qualified candidates interviewed
- Time taken to fill the position from job posting to hire
- Percentage of hiring completed within the planned timeline

—

4. Focus/Other: Raise VC funding

Goal: Raise 1 million EUR from a UK-based VC by June 1st

KPIs:

- Number of pitch meetings held with potential investors
- Amount of funding secured per meeting
- Investor feedback score on pitch presentations

* * *

Key Takeaways

- **The Importance of Goal Setting**: Setting clear goals provides direction, helping you prioritize what matters most. It allows you to track progress, stay accountable, and make data-driven decisions that lead to meaningful results.

- **Create a Simple Plan**: The *Simple Plan* is a streamlined planning method that involves creating a clear, actionable, and flexible plan with measurable goals. It helps entrepreneurs stay focused and on track, while maintaining adaptability to changes and challenges.

- **Goal Alignment for Success**: Aligning your focus areas, financial targets, and actions ensures that every part of your plan contributes to your larger goals. This alignment clarifies priorities and ensures that all team members understand how their efforts support the company's success.

Module 8

Performance Tracking

* * *

Performance tracking naturally follows goal setting. Once your goals are in place, it's essential to monitor your progress by gathering and analyzing financial, sales, and marketing data. These data help you identify opportunities for improvement, make better decisions, and optimize performance, all while keeping your team aligned and focused.

As Peter Drucker famously said, "If you can't measure it, you can't manage it."

As your business scales, the complexity of managing it increases beyond what you can handle based on gut feeling. If you're not equipped with up-to-date

> *"If you can't measure it, you can't manage it."*

insights, adding more clients and staff can lead to chaos and poor execution. Performance tracking gives you a clear snapshot of your operations, allowing you to concentrate on executing the right things rather than feeling overwhelmed by the sheer volume of tasks. This not only leads to greater success, it also helps you become a more effective manager.

Admittedly, performance tracking isn't the most glamorous side of entrepreneurship. Few founders start a business with the dream of perfecting data collection and analysis. But as your business grows, tracking becomes an opportunity, not a burden. The more data you gather, the more trends you can identify, which helps you make informed decisions.

Over time, distinct trends will start to emerge. These patterns, whether in your financial performance, sales, or operational efficiency, will offer valuable insights. For example, if lead generation continually underperforms, it may signal the need to rethink your marketing strategy—for example, by exploring different channels or refining your messaging. Alternatively, you might find that certain expenses regularly go over budget, indicating a need to find savings in other areas or to generate additional revenue to meet your profit targets. Use these patterns as a guide for making informed decisions and adjusting your strategies.

With these insights in mind, it's important to implement a structured approach to performance tracking. In this module, I'll show you how to create a simple, Excel-based system for collecting and evaluating your data. This system will help you draw actionable conclusions and keep your business on the path to growth.

Track Your Financial Results

To effectively manage your finances, it's essential to track your results regularly. You've already established financial goals using a spreadsheet to break down projected monthly revenues, costs, net income, and profit margins. At the start of each month, update this spreadsheet to reflect the actual revenues and costs from the previous period.

When you compare your actual results to your plan, you'll notice small fluctuations each month, both positive and negative.

You will likely expand the level of financial detail you track as your business grows. The more information you gather, the easier it becomes to spot trends, make informed decisions, and continuously improve your financial performance.

Evaluate Your Goals and KPIs

Once a month, review your progress against the goals and related KPIs you set during the goal-setting process. Do the same for your operational KPIs. Make notes about what you've achieved so far, and what still lies ahead. If your goals are measurable, you should be able to make a clear, objective assessment of whether you're on track. For goals that are harder to quantify and require subjective ratings, use your internal judgment to evaluate your progress on a scale of one to ten.

Create a Management Dashboard

You can simplify the evaluation process by creating a management dashboard that consolidates key financial data and KPIs into a single spreadsheet. This summary sheet should include essential metrics such as total monthly revenues, expenses, profits, lead numbers, and conversion rates—providing you with a clear overview of your business's performance.

To ensure accuracy and efficiency, link your management dashboard to the individual spreadsheets tracking your financial results—one each for revenues and costs—and one for your key performance indicators. These connections will keep the dashboard updated automatically and reduce the likelihood of calculation errors. Review this dashboard regularly to spot trends, such as increasing revenues or declining leads, so you identify areas of success and those needing improvement.

Simon Neal, founder of CampMap, has used this approach to make sure he's up-to-speed on his sales and marketing performance. "We do three-month plans, we have revenue targets per month, and now I have a nice system to track it," he reveals.

"You can simplify the evaluation process by creating a management dashboard that consolidates key financial data and KPIs into a single spreadsheet."

Review and Adjust Your Action Plan

Finally, every few weeks, compare your actual progress to the steps outlined in your action plan. Treat this as a dynamic tool that you update frequently: mark completed tasks, remove those that are no longer relevant, and adjust deadlines as needed. It's common to overestimate what can be achieved within a specific timeframe, so be prepared for progress to be slower than anticipated. Although creating a Gantt Chart during the goal-setting process can streamline your review, you can use the same review method even if your action plan is in a document format.

How to Use Performance Information

Having all this information at your disposal is pointless if you don't put it to good use. Dedicate time each month to track your progress and make informed decisions based on a clear understanding of your business's reality. It's essential to accept the data as it is and avoid minimizing poor results or exaggerating successes. Acknowledge that these results collectively represent a snapshot of where your business stands at this moment.

Here are five effective ways to use your performance data:

1. **Fix what's broken**

    If results are disappointing, take a closer look at the numbers and circumstances to identify their root causes. Is it a lack of effort or missed opportunities? This deeper analysis will help you implement corrective actions, keeping you on track and allowing you to adapt to changes in your business or market.

2. **Develop a mini action plan**

    Once you've identified areas for improvement, outline specific steps to address these issues and take immediate action to turn things around. You may need to put more effort into lead generation, adjust your allocation of resources, or cut costs. Addressing issues quickly ensures your business remains aligned with your goals.

3. **Acknowledge what's working**

    Performance tracking isn't just about focusing on the problems. It's also an opportunity to recognize and reward achievements. Celebrating successes and distributing praise, whether individual or team-based, boosts morale and reinforces positive behavior. Even if you're a solopreneur, acknowledging your own efforts is important.

4. **Adjust your expectations**

   You may find that certain goals are no longer as relevant or realistic due to changes in circumstances. It's fine to set them aside or replace them with new priorities. However, avoid revising a goal too quickly just because it feels challenging. Stick with your goals long enough to allow for meaningful progress before adjusting.

5. **Share results with your team**

   Transparency fosters trust. By keeping your team and co-founders informed about the company's performance, you encourage a collaborative environment. Appropriate forums for sharing updates, depending on the size of your organization, may include:

   - Daily fifteen-minute progress reports focusing on key metrics.

   - Weekly or biweekly senior leadership meetings to discuss strategic direction.

   - Monthly or quarterly all-hands meetings to celebrate larger milestones and foster team engagement.

   - Periodic one-on-one performance reviews to provide personalized feedback and guidance.

By regularly reflecting on your strategies and their effectiveness, you can foster a culture of continuous improvement that will benefit your business in the long run.

Bruno Stojakovic, founder of PlaySafety, learned from experience how vital continuous assessment and adjustment are in building a business. Initially targeting hotels, theme parks, and councils with his playground safety software for children's play areas, he found that hotel owners didn't see the value in safety alone, while progress with theme parks was slower than expected. After evaluating his approach, he shifted his focus to city councils, which now make up 75 percent of PlaySafety's client base. As Bruno reflects, "You realize through trial and error what's working and what's not. It's not a straight line—it's a constant process of adjustment and learning."

Tracking Takes Time and Commitment

Remember that the journey toward perfection, which doesn't actually exist, takes time. Begin with simple tasks, gradually increasing the complexity as you become more comfortable with the principles of performance tracking. Don't give up too easily. Consistently monitor results and use data to guide your decisions, striking a balance between intuition and hard numbers.

> *"Begin with simple tasks, gradually increasing the complexity as you become more comfortable with the principles of performance tracking."*

Over time, you'll find it easier to leverage data to either reinforce or challenge your instincts effectively. Resist the temptation to rely solely on gut feelings; instead, trust the insights derived from the data you collect to guide you in the right direction. Make tracking results a regular practice so it becomes an integral part of managing your business. Eventually, this effort will transform your business into a scalable enterprise.

Key Takeaways

- **The Importance of Performance Tracking**: Tracking performance is crucial for monitoring your business's progress, giving you valuable insights into areas needing improvement. It helps you make data-driven decisions, ensuring that your actions are in alignment with your goals and driving success.

- **How to Track Your Performance**: Regularly update key metrics such as financial spreadsheets, sales, and KPIs. Use management dashboards to consolidate these metrics, making it easier to spot trends and assess your progress toward your goals.

- **Using Data to Improve**: Analyze performance data to identify strengths and weaknesses, and take immediate action to address areas for improvement. Share results with your team to foster collaboration, adjust strategies when necessary, and maintain a culture of continuous improvement.

Module 9

Team Development

* * *

As a founder, no matter how brilliant you are, you can't do everything yourself. You can't contact every client, go on every sales call, prepare every proposal, or attend every event. If you want to build a sustainable, scalable business, you must develop a team that can assume some or all of these responsibilities.

In the early stages of your business, it's natural to manage every aspect of sales and marketing yourself, handling all execution and making every decision. While this approach keeps the sales and marketing function relatively straightforward, at some stage it becomes a bottleneck for growth. After all, there are only twenty-four hours in a day and there is only one—or perhaps a few—of you to fill it with meaningful work. Crucially, this shift should be driven by the needs of your growing business, not your discomfort with selling.

Many founders face challenges when it comes to building a team that addresses the organization's skill gaps. Often, they simply lack clear guidelines on how to do this effectively. At the same time, they're hesitant to take the first steps because of a strong emotional attachment to the business, which they see as their baby. However, this reluctance to delegate can create organizational confusion, diminish the quality of execution, and ultimately prevent the startup or professional services provider from reaching their full potential.

To address this, it's essential to recognize your strengths and weaknesses, build a team with the right skills and attitude, and create an environment that enables them to perform at their best. Don't view team development as an all-or-nothing switch where you go from doing everything to delegating everything overnight. Instead, treat it as a gradual process that will transform your role over time. Your goal should be to slowly hand over day-to-day sales and

"Once you've applied these principles, you'll free yourself to work on the business rather than in it."

marketing functions to trusted employees and ultimately delegate full revenue responsibility to a single leader.

In this module, I outline the stages of this transition and introduce guidelines that will ensure your handover runs smoothly. This includes defining key roles, hiring the right mix of employees and freelancers, building a diverse team with a blend of skills and personalities, and introducing best practices for operational excellence.

Once you've applied these principles, you'll free yourself to work *on* the business rather than *in* it, allowing you to focus on long-term strategy and ensuring sustainable growth.

Four Stages of Sales Team Development

Your evolution from a one-man band to an orchestra conductor happens in four stages—each one adds a layer of complexity and effectiveness that enables the development of a scalable organization.

It's unlikely that you can skip any of these levels; instead, you'll need to progress through them step by step.

Level One: Founder-Driven Sales

At the start, you're a jack-of-all-trades, managing all sales and marketing activities. This hands-on involvement allows you to gain vital customer feedback, refine your product, and build strong customer relationships. Avoid outsourcing too soon, as it may lead to missed insights that shape your product or service.

Level Two: Build the Core Team

As your business grows, you'll bring a handful of sales and marketing team members to handle specific functions, such as lead generation, content creation, or customer outreach. While they support your efforts, you'll still be responsible for strategy, execution, and meeting sales targets. At this stage, you're gradually delegating tasks that let you focus on broader goals.

Level Three: Expanding with External Partners

To extend your reach, you may engage external sales agents, distributors, or channel partners. This adds complexity, as you must now manage relationships and performance outside your direct control. Aligning external agents with your internal strategy and ensuring consistent messaging and accountability presents new challenges. Prioritizing clear communication and putting performance metrics in place are key to success at this stage.

Level Four: Appointing a Leader

Eventually, you'll need to hire a dedicated sales and marketing leader—or one for each area of your business—to manage day-to-day operations. This person will handle strategy execution, revenue goals, and team management. Your role will shift to focusing on high-level strategy and addressing key issues, allowing you to concentrate on scaling the business rather than daily operations.

Cover Key Functions and Roles

Below is a list of key sales and marketing functions, with the most common role titles in parentheses. Not all of these functions are necessary from the outset; many will become relevant and

"You will likely need to implement each function eventually to build a strong and scalable sales and marketing organization."

necessary only after you reach specific levels of revenue and organizational maturity. Keep in mind, however, that you will likely need to implement each function eventually to build a strong and scalable sales and marketing organization.

Sales Functions

- Lead Generation (*Sales Development Representative/SDR*): Identifying and qualifying prospects, typically through outreach.

- Account Management (*Account/Sales Executive*): Engaging with qualified leads, creating and presenting proposals, and negotiating deals.

- Partnership Sales (*Partnership/Channel Sales Manager*): Overseeing external sales agents and partnerships, including outreach, contract negotiation, managing relationships.

- Sales Administration (*Sales Assistant*): Handling contracts, billing, CRM updates, and managing sales materials.

- After-Sales Support (*Customer Success*): Ensuring customer satisfaction during onboarding and ongoing product or service use. May include upselling additional services to current customers.

Marketing Functions

- Content Marketing (*Content Producer/Marketer*): Creating and distributing written and video content across social media channels and email newsletters.

- Digital Advertising (*Ad Manager*): Overseeing paid ad campaigns on platforms like Google and social media.

- Public Relations and Events (*PR/Events Coordinator*): Managing media and podcast appearances and organizing the company's presence at events.

- Marketing Partnerships (*Partnerships Manager*): Developing non-sales-focused collaborations with organizations, often in alignment with PR and event strategies.

- Marketing Services (*Graphic Designer, Video Producer*): Handling project-based creative tasks like design, photography, and video production, often in collaboration with content teams.

Fill Roles with the Right Resource

Once you've identified the relevant sales and marketing functions, you must determine the best way to fill these roles.

The number of functions assigned to each person will vary depending on your business's stage of development and available resources. In the early stages, one or two individuals—often the founders—may cover most, if not all, responsibilities. As the company matures, these broad roles typically split into narrower, specialized functions, each eventually overseen by a leader who may be supported by an entire team.

> *"As the company matures, these broad roles typically split into narrower, specialized functions, each eventually overseen by a leader who may be supported by an entire team."*

Fortunately, many of these roles can be filled by part-time or freelance professionals. The shift to hybrid work, accelerated by COVID-19, has led to a vast pool of service providers who prefer working with multiple clients instead of committing to a single full-time employer. Tapping into these resources gives you the flexibility to adjust your team structure as your business evolves, helping you avoid long-term financial commitments until you're confident a specific role is needed, or a candidate is the right fit.

Start by deciding which roles are best suited for full- or part-time employment—this choice will likely depend on both your immediate needs and budget. Then, assess whether a role should be filled by an in-house team member—someone dedicated to your organization—or handled by an external provider. Most likely, you will outsource part-time roles and keep full-time positions in-house.

Biotech scaleup Computomics meets its marketing needs through a team of freelancers handling various functions. A part-time digital marketer manages the content calendar, podcast, blog, and social media. Another part-time specialist oversees events and marketing partnerships, working with sales on conference attendance and maintaining industry association relationships. An external agency supports messaging and website management.

Recommended In-House Roles

Certain functions are foundational to understanding customer needs and maintaining strong relationships, so it's advisable to keep these roles within your organization:

Lead Generation (SDR): This role helps you define and attract your ideal customer, so keep it in-house early on. While many lead generation agencies exist, outsourcing too soon can lead to paying for irrelevant leads before you've clarified your ideal customer profile.

Account Management: Keep this role in-house to stay close to your customers, deeply understand their needs, and foster strong relationships that are essential for client satisfaction and loyalty.

Partnership Sales (Channel Sales Management): Managing external sales agents and channel partners should also be an in-house role, as it requires a deep understanding of your business.

Roles Suitable for Outsourcing

Other functions are less critical to keep in-house, especially in the early stages. These roles can often be managed by external providers or on a part-time basis:

Sales Administration and After-Sales Support: These functions involve operational support, like managing contracts and onboarding, which can typically be outsourced until the volume of customers justifies having full-time hires.

Marketing Functions: Mostly project-based functions like digital advertising, content production, and creative services can be outsourced. As the volume of activity grows, you may want to bring certain functions, like content marketing, in-house. You may also consider hiring an in-house marketing manager to oversee all activities and coordinate freelancers.

Hire a Mix of Skills and Personalities

Building a sales and marketing team for an early-stage business requires a special approach to hiring. It's essential to find candidates with not only the right skills and experience but also the right attitude and tolerance for risk—qualities that are amplified in a startup environment.

Don't focus solely on candidates with impressive credentials or corporate experience; successful startups thrive on proactive self-starters who can problem-solve with limited resources. Those accustomed to structured corporate settings may struggle in a fluid environment, so seek individuals who can create structure and processes rather than rely on established systems. Above all, they must be comfortable with uncertainty.

Richard Basa, CEO and co-founder of low-code application developer Oriana, learned a valuable lesson from scaling with the wrong people. He brought on several senior executives with backgrounds in large tech companies with the aim of professionalizing his operations in sales, marketing, and delivery. Richard soon recognized that while these leaders had deep experience, they struggled to adapt to the

"It's essential to find candidates with not only the right skills and experience but also the right attitude and tolerance for risk."

limited resources and unpredictability of a smaller organization. He ultimately decided to reduce his team and set the company back on a growth path. "We just weren't ready to expand senior management at this stage. It was an expensive misstep," Richard reflects.

Finally, ensure you hire the right person for each role. For instance, a finance manager and a sales manager will approach their work differently; expecting them to operate the same way could hinder productivity. Salespeople often reach for the stars, while data analysts keep their feet on the ground. Recognizing these differences will help you cultivate a balanced and effective team.

If you intend to build a business with international clients, it's vital that all customer-facing team members can speak and write proficiently in English, the de facto language of global business. Any team member who can't speak English, even those with purely internal functions, will find their impact is limited as the business grows. Consider making English the standard for internal communication to promote practice and identify those needing support. Knowledge of other languages—such as German, French, Spanish, Russian, Mandarin, or Arabic—can also be advantageous in specific markets.

While English proficiency is important, hiring individuals from diverse cultural backgrounds is equally valuable. A team with varied perspectives can provide fresh insights and improve your global expansion efforts. Aim to recruit from different countries and cultures, particularly those linked to your target markets. This diversity will enhance your team's ability to navigate and succeed in global business environments.

Create Guidelines for Operating Excellence

Regardless of the number of individuals managing your sales and marketing functions—whether in-house, outsourced, full-time, or part-time—it's essential to establish clear operating guidelines for your organization. This clarity fosters accountability and empowerment, driving team effectiveness and accelerating company growth.

Build a Product Knowledge Hub: Ensure every member of your team has a comprehensive understanding of your product, its value proposition, and strategic direction. Create a folder with company presentations, product information, and marketing materials that they access when they join the company and can refer to on an ongoing basis. Regularly update these materials to reflect the latest developments.

Clarify Individual Responsibilities: Ensure each team member has a clear understanding of their specific responsibilities. Outline the key tasks and objectives associated with their role, addressing any questions they may have. Document these responsibilities to create a shared reference that reinforces expectations and accountability, helping to align the team's efforts toward common goals.

Define Success Metrics: Make sure each team member knows how their work will be evaluated. If you've followed the goal-setting principles outlined earlier, each employee should clearly understand their performance criteria. For instance, account management can be evaluated by revenue generation, after-sales support by upsells, content marketing by engagement levels, and partnerships by the number and quality of deals secured.

Set Decision-Making Authority: Ensure everyone knows what they can and can't decide. Early on, founders approve almost all decisions, but as the organization grows, the decision-making process needs to evolve. Empower those closest to a problem to make relevant decisions—for example, allowing an account manager to handle client issues. This approach builds a team of accountable, empowered individuals, accelerating company growth.

Hold Regular Check-Ins: Develop a schedule for regular one-on-one meetings to discuss performance, provide feedback, address challenges, and share insights. As your organization grows, schedule a recurring weekly or biweekly meeting where functional heads can share information with you and each other, and you brainstorm joint decisions. Frequent communication helps build a stronger working relationship, ensures accountability, and keeps each member of your team aligned with your evolving strategy.

* * *

Key Takeaways

- **Build a Scalable Team**: Building a strong team is vital for sustainable business growth. A well-structured team allows founders to focus on long-term strategy, delegating operational tasks and ensuring scalability as the business expands.

- **Stages of Sales Team Development**: The transition from founder-driven sales to a fully managed sales team happens in four stages, starting with hands-on involvement and evolving into leadership roles. This gradual shift allows founders to delegate, ultimately empowering one leader to take full responsibility for sales and marketing.

- **Best Practices for Team Building**: To build an effective sales and marketing team, founders should focus on key functions, hire the right mix of internal and external resources, and ensure the right skills and attitude. Clear guidelines, regular check-ins, and measurable success metrics foster accountability and drive growth.

From Founding to Scaling

* * *

You know you're ready to scale your business when certain positive and negative signals are impossible to ignore. On the one hand, you sense traction with customers: deals are closing, and momentum is building. Your team feels the energy of growth, and opportunities seem to be coming faster than you can handle.

On the flip side, cracks in your operations begin to appear. Tracking progress becomes harder, your to-do list grows longer, and early employees or co-founders start stepping on each other's toes. Missed deadlines and confusion creep in, leaving you

"To scale effectively, you must shift from a founding mindset to a scaling mindset."

feeling overwhelmed. At this point, something has to change—either your business adapts, or it risks stagnation.

To scale effectively, you must shift from a founding mindset to a scaling mindset.

Start by setting clear, measurable goals. Without defined targets, your team's efforts lack direction and growth stalls. Align these goals with your broader vision and daily operations. Next, implement performance tracking tools to identify what's working and what isn't. Regular reviews will help you spot trends and make data-driven decisions. Finally, clarify roles and responsibilities within your team. Empower individuals by assigning ownership and hiring specialists to fill gaps in expertise.

This process is iterative and unfolds over time. By mastering these elements, you create a scalable foundation, allowing you to focus on growth, support your team, and shift from daily firefighting to strategic growth.

Antavo: Scaling to Industry Leadership

Antavo is a customer loyalty SaaS technology that struggled for years to find product-market fit. Led by co-founders Attila and Zsuzsa Kecsmar, the company pivoted multiple times before ultimately becoming an industry-agnostic solution for enterprise-level customers. Today, Antavo powers the loyalty programs of global brands like KFC, C&A, Scandic Hotels, and Benefit Cosmetics across four continents.

What's even more remarkable than its commercial evolution— which I witnessed firsthand as an early advisor, investor, and now chairman—is how Antavo scaled its operations to meet the demands of its growing business.

The company's organizational development unfolded in stages. Initially a small team, it grew to twelve employees, with co-founder Andy Nemes as the sole salesperson, plus a dedicated writer and graphic designer for early marketing efforts. After securing €1.3 million in seed funding, Antavo transitioned from purely founder-led selling to employing a broader, more experienced team of salespeople. The company grew to forty people, adding an experienced sales leader, solution consultants, and strategists to handle more complex deals. This period saw the introduction of critical processes like lead qualification, reporting, and commission structures, laying the foundation for scalable, data-driven growth.

As the team expanded to include employees who'd worked at larger organizations, so did the need for goal setting and planning. Antavo introduced Objectives and Key Results (OKR) to align individual contributions with company goals. As Attila explains, "At first, I didn't fully grasp why OKRs mattered, but once we got it right, we realized that aligning individual contributions with company goals drove shared success and increased transparency across the team."

By the time the team grew to 120, the founders' roles had evolved: a professional sales leader took over for co-founder Andy, who shifted his focus to generating new business in the US. Zsuzsa leads a robust marketing and partnerships team and has become the de facto face of the company. Attila, as CEO, shifted from product management to high-level strategy and innovation, and co-founder Gabor Csarnai has remained focused on technology without leadership duties.

Antavo's organizational evolution shows how redesigning operations is critical to scaling a business into a global industry leader.

PART 3

TACTICS

I once heard about a startup founder who, believing email marketing was the golden ticket to success, launched a massive campaign to thousands of potential leads. With a polished design and an eye-catching subject line, he confidently hit "send"—only to realize hours later that every link in his email led recipients to a pornography site, not his intended landing page.

While this might sound like a worst-case scenario, it's far from isolated. This level of execution failure is a shocking reminder: no matter how brilliant your strategy, it's worth nothing if you don't get the details right. The real danger? This kind of blunder can undo months—or even years—of hard work in a single click.

It's critical to choose the right tactics—those specific, actionable steps that produce real-time results—when executing your sales and marketing strategy. Each day presents these high-stakes opportunities, and the decisions you make in these micro-moments can be the difference between success and failure:

- Should I engage with this prospect or are they wasting my time?

- How can I reconnect with the distributor I spoke to at an industry event?

- When should I introduce an automation tool to reach out to target customers?

While the wrong move can waste valuable time and resources, getting it right propels you forward and sets the stage for exponential growth.

This final section equips you with key tactics to navigate the most common scenarios in the early stages of your sales journey. Inside, you'll find actionable frameworks and immediately implementable advice to drive results. Plus, I'll introduce you to two powerful exercises—the *Destination Plan* and *Blast Off! Blueprint*—that will help you identify the most impactful steps to reach your goals faster.

Follow these tactics and you'll not only master execution, but you'll successfully implement *The Launch Code* in your business.

CHAPTER 6

Navigating Real-World Scenarios

"In theory, theory and practice are the same.
In practice, they are not."
– Dr. Albert Einstein

Throughout this book, I've shared the mindset and strategies that have helped hundreds of tech founders and professional service providers to accelerate their revenue growth. Yet, experience has shown that once you start applying these strategies in the real world, unexpected challenges arise. There's always a gap between theory and practice, even though managing these difficulties is a natural part of the sales journey.

To help you navigate these sales obstacles, I've compiled the most common issues founders face and provide actionable steps to tackle them. While there will inevitably be moments when you feel uncertain or caught off guard, remember that with each hurdle you overcome, the process becomes easier.

Sales Activities

How to Use LinkedIn for Outreach

LinkedIn is essential for B2B sales, enabling you to build relationships with target customers and strengthen your industry credibility. If you're serious about growing your network, you must keep your LinkedIn profile updated and engage actively with target clients via the platform.

> *"If you're serious about growing your network, you must keep your LinkedIn profile updated and engage actively with target clients via the platform."*

Personal Profile: include a clear value proposition in your profile headline and banner. In the "About" section, highlight the problem your business solves, who it serves, and why your solution stands out. Use the "Featured" section to link to your website, lead magnets, or other credibility-boosting content. This ensures people see why your connection request may be relevant to them.

Company Profile: Create a company page to enhance your legitimacy and make it easier for prospects to find your business via search engines. Keep in mind, however, that while your connections can follow your company page, you can only send connection requests via your personal profile.

Your Networking Approach: When engaging with target customers on LinkedIn, avoid the "pitch slap"—sending overly sales-focused messages right away. Treat LinkedIn networking like in-person networking: just as you wouldn't immediately pitch to someone you meet at an event, focus on building rapport first. Take the time to understand your connection's needs before discussing potential collaboration. The goal is to foster genuine virtual conversations that naturally lead to opportunities where you can demonstrate how your solution meets their needs.

Marton Demeter, founder of property maintenance company HMMConsultant, used LinkedIn effectively to connect with property managers in London. He started with a personalized, non-salesy connection request, highlighting shared interests. After acceptance, he sent a thank-you message and shared free resources like "Top 10 Tips for Easy Refurbishment" to build trust and demonstrate expertise. To enhance his credibility, he provided case studies of his work with two industry-leading companies before inviting prospects to a meeting to discuss his services.

Connection Requests: Personalize your connection request only if there's a clear, relevant connection such as a close mutual contact or if you've already met in person. This will help build familiarity and establish a context for your outreach. Avoid generic messages like "I'm reaching out because I'm expanding my network." Instead, send your connection request without a message. Once your request is accepted, your posts will be more likely to appear in your new contact's feed, helping you to stay top of their mind. You'll also be able to send personalized follow-up messages that help build a relationship.

Engagement and Follow-Up: After your connection request is accepted, thank your new contact and periodically share relevant content or ask about challenges your product addresses. Over time, you'll either receive a response indicating interest or be told your offering isn't relevant. In most cases, you won't get a reply, but once you get at least two positive responses or engagements, ask if they'd like to learn how your solution helped a company like theirs. If they express interest, ask some qualifying questions and/or suggest a video chat or meeting.

How to Manage a Discovery Call

A discovery call is an introductory conversation aimed at understanding a prospect's business, challenges, and goals, and assessing whether your product or service can meet their needs. Don't try to close a deal right away. Instead, focus on building rapport, asking questions, presenting your solution, and setting the stage for a product demo or proposal. Ultimately, this call allows both parties to evaluate the potential for further engagement.

Preparing for Your Call: To make the most of your conversation, research the prospect's business, industry, and any challenges they likely face. Review their LinkedIn profile, company website, and articles to gather intel. By doing your homework, you'll not only make a good first impression, but you'll be more confident and effective in guiding the conversation toward a productive outcome.

Set Expectations and Agenda: Avoid jumping straight into a pitch. Begin by outlining the agenda for the call: first, you'd like to understand your prospect's challenges; next, you'll share your solution and examples of companies you've helped; third, you explain how—if there's a fit—you'd be able to work together. Finally, you'll decide together whether it makes sense to continue the conversation.

Ask Probing Questions: To understand your prospect's business and pain points, begin with open-ended questions such as:

- Can you tell me a bit about your business?

- What is your biggest business challenge right now?

- What prompted you to reach out to me?

- What are you hoping to achieve in the next six to twelve months?

As the conversation progresses, follow up with targeted questions to uncover underlying challenges your potential client often faces. These questions show genuine interest while offering valuable insights to tailor your pitch. You might discover details that highlight the urgency of their problem or reveal a new perspective, helping you address their specific pain points and demonstrate how your solution fits.

Prospects will most likely want to discuss their challenges first, especially if they've reached out for help. If a prospect pushes for an immediate presentation of your product, resist the urge to dive in. Instead, share a brief overview, if necessary, then pivot back to asking questions to fully understand their needs.

Present Your Solution: Once you're confident your solution aligns with the prospect's needs, summarize the challenges they've shared and explain how these are similar to those your clients faced before using your product or service. By drawing a clear connection between their pain points and your solution, you make your prospect feel heard and demonstrate your understanding.

Next, present your value proposition and explain how your product or service addresses your prospect's specific challenges. Link your product's features and benefits directly to the issues your prospect has shared. Illustrate your solution with case studies or examples from clients who faced similar challenges, especially those in the same industry or region. Highlighting the positive results you've achieved for them will help build credibility and trust in your solution.

Finally, present your product offering and suggest a process whereby they can evaluate your offer and arrive at an agreement. Depending on what you're selling, the next step might be to organize a product demo or a follow-up meeting with other stakeholders, or it may jump directly to sending a proposal.

> *"Handling objections is a natural part of the buying process, so it's important to be prepared to answer them."*

Pause occasionally to check for understanding or ask if they have any questions. This keeps them engaged and reinforces your connection throughout the meeting.

Handle Objections: As you present your solution, it's likely you'll encounter objections, often in the form of questions. This is a natural part of the buying process, so it's important to be prepared to answer them. Typical questions might include:

- How does your solution work?

- What makes your solution different from others?

- What kind of results can I expect, and how soon?

- How do you justify the cost of your product?

To address objections effectively, use the following three steps:

- **Repeat**: Reflect back the prospect's concern to indicate that you've understood their objection.

- **Reframe**: Shift their perspective on the problem ("$1,000 per month is a fraction of what you'll save if you introduce our product.") or provide new information that gives them comfort ("Our business may be only two years old, but our founding team has fifteen years of professional experience in the industry.").

- **Reinforce**: Reaffirm that your solution is the best fit for solving their problem.

For example, if a prospect questions the cost of your meeting management training program, especially since they previously invested in productivity programs that didn't deliver value, you could respond like this:

- **Repeat**: "I understand that you've invested in other training programs in the past that didn't meet your expectations, and you're concerned about wasting money."

- **Reframe**: "But think about the cost of unproductive meetings. If your team spent less time in those meetings and more time managing projects or engaging with customers, you could significantly boost productivity. For example, if you calculate the salary of ten employees at an average of €3,000 per month, that's €360,000 in lost productivity annually. Our program costs only €3,000, less than one month's salary for one person, and the return is improved productivity for a whole year."

- **Reinforce**: "This investment will not only bring long-lasting benefits, but it's one of the smartest decisions you'll make for your team."

Over time, you'll become familiar with the most common objections, and you can refine your responses. Keep a log of these objections and how you addressed them, so you're always prepared for future conversations.

Qualify and Agree Next Steps: As you conduct a meeting, make sure you continually assess whether your prospect is appropriate for your solution (See "How to Qualify a Prospect"). If at any moment you feel they don't meet your qualification criteria, politely wrap up the call. If you reach the end of the meeting and you believe your prospect is a good fit, ask them if they'd like to continue the process. If so, try to schedule the next meeting immediately. If they're unable to commit, clearly outline the next steps and timelines—whether that includes a follow-up email, product demo, or proposal preparation. Always end the call with a mutual understanding of what happens next and a qualified assessment of the prospect's interest.

Manage Your Time: A typical discovery call lasts around thirty minutes, so you must manage your time to fit the entire process into this time frame. Make sure to set aside five minutes for introductions and technical checks and reserve the last five minutes to confirm the next steps. With only twenty minutes to ask questions, present your solution, and handle objections, you must keep a close eye on the clock so you don't end the call without a clear understanding of what happens next.

How to Qualify a Prospect

When assessing the fit of a potential B2B customer, it's important to evaluate both qualitative and quantitative factors to determine whether they are a good match for your product or service. Using these criteria will save you time and resources and help you focus on prospects that are more likely to convert.

Colm Brennan, co-founder of TrakPro—a SaaS platform that streamlines subcontractor payments and tracks project changes in the construction industry—found that qualifying customers was his biggest challenge. Initially, he spent too much time engaging with the wrong prospects. He now focuses on construction companies with enough subcontractors to feel the pain his platform solves, along with an upcoming project on which the customer can test his solution. This shift has speeded up conversations and helped him close his first three deals.

Here are the typical qualification criteria:

- **Problem/Need**: *Do they have a clear need for your solution?*
  If the prospect's pain point is not relevant, they won't buy.

- **Urgency**: *Are the prospect's pain points acute enough to justify a solution?*
  If the prospect's challenges aren't urgent or significant, your discussion will have no momentum.

- **Timing**: *When do they need the solution?*
  Understand their timeline to help you determine if they're in a buying cycle or just exploring options.

- **Budget**: *Do they have the budget to invest in your solution?*
  Understand their financial capacity to help gauge whether they can afford your offering.

- **Decision-Making Authority**: *Are you speaking with the decision-maker or influencer?*
  Ensure you're engaging with someone in a leadership role or with budget authority.

- **Buying Process**: *What does their purchasing process look like?*
  Assess whether the prospect has a formal process for making purchasing decisions, and if this aligns with your sales cycle.

- **Company Fit**: *Does the company size, industry, or market align with your ICP?*
  Make sure you're speaking with a prospect who fits the profile of your ideal customer.

- **Competition**: *Are they considering other competitors or solutions?*
  Understand whether they are comparing other providers or have a preferred vendor.

- **Technical Compatibility**: *Does your solution integrate with their technology stack?*
  Understand their existing systems and ensure your solution can seamlessly integrate with their current software or infrastructure.

- **Cultural Fit**: *Do they share similar values and working styles?*
  Assess compatibility, especially if your product requires close collaboration.

- **Long-Term Potential**: *Is this a potential long-term customer?*
  Consider whether the prospect has the potential to become a strategic partner, or has potential for upselling, cross-selling, or expansion within the organization.

How to Negotiate an Agreement

Don't approach negotiation as a win/lose proposition. Both parties should walk away feeling that they contributed what they were comfortable with and received enough to make the deal worthwhile. If your goal is to outsmart the other party, even if you do manage to get a short-term win, you're unlikely to build a beneficial, long-term relationship.

Know **Your Negotiation Goal**: Start each negotiation knowing what you want to achieve. For example, it might be to close your first deal so you can begin testing your product and gather user feedback. Alternatively, you may already have enough clients, so you can focus on raising prices, or accessing a new market segment or geographical area.

Identify Beneficial Compromises: Look for areas where you can be flexible—such as pricing, payment terms, additional services, or performance guarantees. While ensuring fair compensation is important, understanding the other party's priorities helps you find mutually beneficial solutions. For instance, some clients may value a fast turnaround more than cost, while others might prefer a discount in exchange for a longer timeline. Avoid giving in on everything out of eagerness to close the

> *"If your goal is to outsmart the other party, even if you do manage to get a short-term win, you're unlikely to build a beneficial, long-term relationship."*

deal, but don't be so rigid that you miss opportunities for mutual benefit. Be open to compromise on some aspects if it allows you to meet the client's expectations on others, ensuring a win-win outcome.

Develop Boundaries Over Time: As you gain experience and establish a strong track record of successful deals, you'll develop a clearer sense of where you're unwilling to compromise. For example, you might set a minimum price threshold and stand firm, even if it means walking away from a deal that doesn't meet your standards. Over time, you may decide to offer a defined set of options, terms, and conditions—as outlined in the Product Offering module—and eliminate negotiation altogether.

Confirm and Summarize the Agreement: After reaching an agreement, confirm it via email to avoid misunderstandings and proceed with drafting the contract. Share a summary of the next steps, especially for long delivery timelines, to ensure clarity. This helps manage expectations, fosters a sense of continuity, and keeps both parties engaged.

How to Sell to Corporations

Landing a deal with a large corporation is a major milestone for most startups. Such a partnership brings substantial revenue, enhances credibility, and opens doors to similar organizations. Securing corporate clients, however, is fraught with challenges. Corporate sales cycles can stretch to twelve or even eighteen months, a daunting timeline for startups with lean budgets and tight schedules. The process can feel like navigating a maze, with new gatekeepers, complex internal politics, and unexpected roadblocks at every turn.

But the challenges don't end with the deal. During the delivery phase, corporate structures and slow-moving processes can delay execution, leaving founders accustomed to quick decisions frustrated by bureaucracy.

The clash between startup and corporate mentalities stems from their fundamentally different approaches to risk and decision-making. Startups thrive on uncertainty, valuing speed and rapid decision-making to stay competitive, while corporations prioritize risk avoidance and slow, committee-driven processes. In the corporate world, the stakes are higher, and decision-makers often resist new solutions due to internal politics and fear of risk. This behavior is deeply ingrained in corporate DNA.

To succeed in corporate sales, startups must first accept the nature of corporate decision-making and set realistic expectations for what is possible. With patience and preparation, founders can successfully steer the process and negotiate an agreement. You can boost your chances by focusing on the right corporate targets, aligning your solution with their needs, and taking a resourceful approach.

Target "Deer" not "Elephants"

Not all corporations are equally suited for doing business with a startup. While large corporations may seem intimidating, it's helpful to remember the principle of hunting "deer," not "elephants." Instead of targeting the biggest players, focus on smaller yet significant companies—often challengers that occupy second or third place in their market. These companies are more likely to embrace innovative ideas that can give them a competitive edge.

The most promising "deer" share certain characteristics that indicate a willingness to explore new solutions and take calculated risks. Privately held companies tend to be more open to innovation since they don't face the same shareholder pressures as those traded on the stock market, which are more conservative and hesitant to invest without immediate financial returns. The best targets also have a corporate startup accelerator, operate a corporate venture capital fund, and employ someone whose job title is "Head of Innovation" or something similar.

Once you've identified your targets, it's typically more effective to reach out to the company's headquarters rather than to a subsidiary.

Subsidiaries often lack the authority to approve new innovations, so even if you win their interest, they may be unable to move forward with approval from their headquarters.

Apply These Success Boosters

You can significantly increase your chances of closing a corporate deal by following certain tactics:

Present High-Impact Solutions: Position your product or service as a must-have that solves a critical problem or delivers significant benefits to a core area of the business. Corporate decision-makers are more likely to explore solutions offering high-impact results, such as a 10 percent revenue boost or cost reductions, rather than smaller, less tangible benefits like improving employee engagement. Even if the benefits of your solution appear gradually, delivering a major win will justify the effort each party puts in to close the deal.

Build Trust Gradually: It's essential to build credibility with decision-makers and influencers. Mention existing corporate clients and highlight your personal corporate experience, if you have either. Show up on time to meetings, follow up as agreed, and deliver high-quality documents and presentations that include relevant KPIs and data. Dress professionally for in-person or virtual meetings.

Highlight Your Stability: Corporations need reassurance that you will be around to fulfill your deal and provide ongoing support. For instance, a car manufacturer developing a new model might rely on technology partnerships that must service models for ten years or more. Share details about your resources, growth plans, and funding to demonstrate your stability and long-term viability.

Cultivate an Internal Champion: Navigating the internal structure of a corporation can be challenging, so an internal champion—someone with authority and influence—can greatly improve your chances of success. This person can help guide you through the decision-making process, identify key stakeholders, and navigate any internal politics. Understanding who makes the decisions, who influences them, and the budgeting process will make it easier for you to position your solution effectively and increase your chances of closing the deal.

Propose a Paid Pilot Project: Consider offering a *paid* pilot project if you feel it's essential to gain traction. A pilot allows corporations to test your solution on a smaller scale, reducing their risk and giving you a chance to prove your value. Avoid a free test period. Charging for the pilot shows your solution has value and ensures the client is invested in the project's success, as well. This fosters accountability and paves the way for a long-term partnership.

Marketing Practices

How to Efficiently Create Content

As a reminder, inbound marketing content is typically divided into three categories: *attract*, *nurture*, and *convert*, corresponding to the top, middle, and bottom of the sales funnel. Top-of-funnel content aims to engage a broad audience, introducing them to your brand and generating awareness. Middle-of-funnel content showcases your expertise and builds relationships with individuals who are aware of their problem and seek a solution. Bottom-of-funnel content encourages prospects to act, like schedule a meeting or purchase a product. To be most effective, focus on 40 percent attract content, 40 percent nurture content, and 20 percent convert content. This balance helps you provide value while guiding prospects toward becoming clients.

Generate Fresh Content Ideas

Generating content ideas for social media, newsletters, and blogs can be challenging, but it gets easier with practice. Stay alert for inspiration in both business and everyday life. I recommend keeping a file on your phone, organized by content type (attract, nurture, and convert), so you can quickly jot down ideas as they come to you. Industry articles or social media posts can spark new ideas or offer opportunities to share your unique perspective.

Additionally, conversations with prospects, customers, and partners often reveal real-life challenges that you can address in your content, making them a valuable source of inspiration. For example, a discussion I had with a conference organizer about an upcoming event where I was scheduled to speak led to a social media post about how to handle business conflicts.

If you stay open to the world around you, you'll find that ideas naturally emerge from your daily experiences. This mindset will prevent you from facing the dreaded blank screen and help you consistently create relevant and engaging content.

Schedule Writing and Publishing

Consistency is key to maximizing the impact of your content. Use a monthly content calendar to plan social media posts and newsletters in advance. This ensures that content creation continues smoothly during busy periods and helps you maintain a balanced mix of topics. Set aside dedicated time each week or month to create content for the upcoming period, allowing you to stay ahead of schedule and keep your posts varied.

Post on social media at least once a week—ideally three times a week—to maintain momentum and visibility. Every post should start with a compelling hook to grab attention and include a relevant image to make it stand out in social media feeds. For newsletters, craft a subject line that entices readers to open it.

On LinkedIn, posts from your personal profile tend to generate more engagement—

"Consistency is key to maximizing the impact of your content."

likes, comments, and shares—than from a company page. Users prefer interacting with individuals, and the platform's algorithm favors personal posts, boosting their reach. This creates better opportunities for lead generation and relationship-building.

How to Collect Testimonials

Customer endorsements play a crucial role in your content strategy, helping to build trust and influence prospects' perceptions. Testimonials are particularly effective in showing that your solution works.

There are two types of testimonials: generic praise and those with specific, measurable results. While both are valuable, testimonials that highlight tangible outcomes, such as increased revenue or customer growth, are especially persuasive. For example, I regularly share charts demonstrating how applying *The Launch Code* generated significant growth in the revenue for specific clients to build credibility with founders.

Case studies take this a step further, offering a detailed narrative that walks potential clients through a customer's challenges, your solutions, and the measurable results achieved. This deeper dive builds trust and showcases your expertise in ways that testimonials alone cannot.

To build a strong library of testimonials and case studies, actively gather feedback from satisfied clients. Organize conversations or send out questionnaires asking about the challenges they faced before working with you, the solutions you provided, and the results they achieved. Whenever possible, include details about other products they considered and why they chose yours, as well as the value they received. Strong, memorable statements, like "You took the voodoo out of sales and marketing," will make your testimonials more impactful.

Finally, catalog your testimonials and use them consistently across social media, your website, and promotional materials. Edit videos into short, compelling clips or highlight powerful quotes to maximize their effect.

How to Prepare for an Event

Attending business events is a great way to expand your network, providing invaluable opportunities to connect with potential clients, partners, and collaborators. Choose events that align with your industry, expertise, or business interests. Try to attend at least two to three events per year, keeping in mind both time and budget constraints.

To reiterate, events offer five main ways to participate: as an attendee, exhibitor, panel member, speaker, or expert (often via a fireside chat). While attending and exhibiting are straightforward options, securing a spot as a panelist or speaker can greatly enhance your impact. Simply being on stage adds authority and visibility.

Preparation is essential to maximizing your event experience. Start by reviewing the speaker list in advance to identify potential partners. Reach out to fellow speakers on LinkedIn with a brief message like, "I see you're also speaking at X event—let's connect!" This simple approach can lead to meaningful connections. Many events also offer apps that allow you to search for attendees by industry and interests, helping you connect before the event and schedule meetings on-site. After connecting through the app, follow up with a LinkedIn connection request to solidify the relationship.

Keep track of everyone you meet, noting whether they are potential clients, partners, or leads for future speaking opportunities. After the event, keep the momentum going by following up promptly—ideally within twenty-four hours—to reinforce the connection and continue the conversation. A simple message acknowledging the meeting and expressing interest in staying in touch can make a big impact.

Timely follow-up demonstrates that you value the connection and boosts the chances of turning initial meetings into long-term business relationships. If there's potential for further collaboration, share relevant content, such as articles or website links. I've often had founders I met at an event reach out to me months later indicating their interest in learning more about my services.

Operational Tips

How to Hold Productive Meetings

I'm not a fan of the anti-meeting culture. It's become trendy to dismiss meetings as timewasters, but that's usually due to poor organization and lack of focus. Meetings don't have to be this way. When they're purposeful, well-structured, and action-driven, they can be a powerful tool for productivity.

Follow these three meeting management principles:

Define a Purpose and Agenda: Every meeting should start with a clearly defined purpose and agenda. Whether you're discussing next quarter's marketing strategy or resolving a product issue, everyone should know why they're there and what needs to be accomplished. Sharing an agenda in advance ensures critical topics are not overlooked and that all agenda items are covered.

Limit Attendance: Only those directly contributing to the meeting's purpose should attend. Ideally, keep attendance to five or fewer, as larger groups often gravitate away from conversations and into presentation mode, which can disengage participants. Smaller meetings encourage active participation, allowing everyone to contribute meaningfully.

Summarize Decisions and Next Steps: Conclude each meeting with a verbal recap of decisions and next steps, assigning action items with deadlines to specific individuals. Follow up with an email summarizing these points to reinforce accountability and provide a foundation for future discussions. Without concrete outcomes, meetings can easily fade into vague brainstorming sessions, but a clear summary ensures momentum and continuity.

How to Use Software Tools

It's a good idea to integrate software tools into your sales and marketing workflow to boost your productivity. These are typically SaaS platforms that require a monthly or annual subscription.

While there are limitless options, I recommend starting with a few basic tools and gradually adding more as you become more comfortable with them and can afford to do so. Over time, your goal should be to build a comprehensive tech stack that supports your most critical sales and marketing activities.

"I recommend starting with a few basic tools and gradually adding more as you become more comfortable with them and can afford to do so."

Below is a list of generic sales tools, along with ones specifically designed for LinkedIn. While categorized by their primary functions, many SaaS platforms offer a mix of features and serve multiple purposes. Some tools may be a better fit for your needs, depending on the combination of features you require. These platforms also offer different pricing plans to suit various needs and budgets.

Be sure to do your own research and take advantage of free trials to test each tool before making a commitment. Keep in mind that switching platforms later can become more difficult as your business grows, so make thoughtful choices upfront.

Basic

- **Appointment Scheduling**: Automates scheduling by displaying available time slots for others to book appointments in real-time. *Examples: Acuity Scheduling, Calendly, YouCanBook.me*

- **Cloud Storage**: Enables management of files and data over the internet, eliminating the need for local storage devices. *Examples: Dropbox, Google Drive, OneDrive*

- **Content Management System**: Allows users to create, manage, and publish digital content on websites without needing extensive technical knowledge. *Examples: Hubspot CMS, Wix, WordPress*

- **Customer Relationship Manager (CRM)**: Helps users manage and analyze interactions with current and potential customers to improve sales. *Examples: Hubspot, Pipedrive, Salesforce*

- **Email Marketing**: Provides tools for creating, sending, and automating email campaigns, managing lists, tracking performance, and segmenting audiences. *Examples: ActiveCampaign, Mailchimp, MailerLite*

- **Social Media Management**: Helps schedule, manage, and analyze social media content across multiple platforms from one interface. *Examples: Buffer, Hootsuite, Sprout Social*

- **Video Conferencing**: Enables users to hold meetings, webinars, and client discovery calls via online video communication. *Examples: Google Meet, Microsoft Teams, Zoom*

Advanced

- **Billing and Subscription Management**: Helps manage recurring billing, invoices, and subscription models to streamline financial operations. *Examples: Chargebee, Recurly, Stripe Billing*

- **Business Intelligence (BI) and Analytics**: Helps track sales performance, customer behavior, and other business metrics to improve decision-making. *Examples: Tableau, Looker, Power BI*

- **Document Management and E-signature**: Helps users to sign, send, and manage documents digitally, streamlining contract and agreement execution. *Examples: DocuSign, HelloSign, PandaDoc*

- **Graphic Design**: Enables users to create visual content like social media posts, presentations, and marketing materials using intuitive templates and tools. *Examples: Adobe Express, Canva, VistaCreate*

- **Project Management**: Facilitates team collaboration, tracking progress, and managing complex workflows within your business. *Examples: Asana, Trello, Monday.com*

- **Sales Enablement**: Equips sales teams with the resources, content, and training they need to close deals more efficiently. *Examples: Seismic, Outreach, SalesLoft*

- **Sales Funnel Builder**: Helps create and optimize sales funnels by building landing pages, lead capture forms, and automating email marketing and checkout. *Examples: ClickFunnels, Kartra, Leadpages*

- **Team Collaboration**: Enables real-time messaging, file sharing, and collaboration, improving team communication and efficiency. *Examples: Chanty, Flock, Slack*

- **Website Analytics:** Helps businesses collect data and analyze user behavior on their website. *Examples: Google Analytics, Hotjar, Mixpanel*

LinkedIn Focused

- **Automation Tools:** Streamlines connecting with prospects, sending messages, and endorsing skills to improve lead generation. These tools carry the risk of detection, so set usage limits to avoid violations of platform policies. *Examples: Dux-Soup, LinkedInHelper, MeetAlfred*

- **Sales Navigator**: Helps users find, connect with, and engage potential leads on LinkedIn through advanced search filters, personalized outreach, and detailed insights on prospects.

- **ShieldApp**: An analytics and reporting tool designed to help users track, measure, and optimize content performance, and gather audience insights on LinkedIn.

- **Surfe**: A sales productivity tool that automates tasks like syncing LinkedIn contacts to CRMs, enriching data, and managing outreach more efficiently.

- **Taplio**: A content management tool that helps generate LinkedIn content, schedule posts, engage with other creators, and measure performance.

How to Expand Internationally

Expanding internationally can help you gain new customers, build your credibility, and generate a higher exit value. Diving into global markets without a clear strategy, however, can lead to wasted resources and hinder progress. Success lies in balancing planning with execution—allocating resources wisely while pursuing quick wins to build momentum.

International growth strategies follow two models: the "Day One Global" or the "Market by Market" approaches. Your business model determines which is the best fit.

Day One Global: Product-led businesses targeting a global audience from launch. These companies use scalable inbound marketing strategies to reach customers across multiple regions, focusing on testing and iteration rather than singular geographic focus.

Market by Market: Businesses following this model focus on achieving product-market fit in one market before expanding. Being close to early customers allows for fast adaptation, minimizing costly errors. This strategy relies on outbound sales and building local partnerships to gain credibility and traction.

If no single market stands out, leverage existing connections—such as a client, partnership, or your network—as a springboard for further expansion.

Emi Gal, co-founder of the US-based medtech startup Ezra, shares a key lesson from his experience of growing internationally with his first business, the adtech tool Brainient. Reflecting on his expansion from the UK into France and Russia, he advises, "Focus on a single market initially, dominate it, and only then move to another market."

Get Prepared and Focused

First, evaluate three key factors: ambition, commitment, and resources. Are you aiming for regional, continental, or global growth? Do you and your team have the capacity to travel or relocate? Ensure you have the operational and financial resources to support expansion.

> *"International expansion will likely demand customized strategies for positioning, market entry, and organizational structure."*

Then, understand that international expansion will likely demand customized strategies for positioning, market entry, and organizational structure.

Refine Your Positioning: Conduct market research to identify your product's value. Evaluate the competition by studying their customer base, pricing strategies, and funding levels to uncover gaps and opportunities. Revisit your value proposition and product offering and refine your messaging to resonate with the local audiences.

Customize Your Market Entry: Use a mix of outbound sales to target key customers, partnerships to build credibility, and inbound marketing to attract customers organically. Start with short-term goals, such as closing two to three deals, to validate your product's fit and build initial momentum for long-term growth.

Strengthen Your Team: Assign a dedicated team to manage expansion and equip them with the tools and knowledge to navigate cross-border sales and marketing. Establish processes that ensure seamless product or service delivery, minimizing disruptions for new customers.

Follow this Execution Blueprint

Once your strategy is clear, follow these steps to guide your journey:

1. **Pick Three Markets**: Choose markets with the right balance of potential, competition, and ease of entry.

2. **Build Local Insights and Relationships**: Attend trade shows, meet contacts, and leverage networks to gather intelligence.

3. **Identify Ten Target Customers or Partners per Market**: Develop a focused list and find meaningful ways to engage with them.

4. **Close Deals and Build Traction**: Secure early wins with customers or partners to validate your strategy.

5. **Establish a Local Presence**: Hire local reps or relocate key team members to support growth.

6. **Support Sales with Targeted Marketing**: Boost credibility with tailored content, events, and PR.

7. **Track Progress and Adapt**: Continuously refine your product offering, messaging, and strategy based on market feedback.

By following these steps, you can systematically expand into international markets, build credibility, and set your startup up for long-term success.

Expanding into international markets requires strategic focus and flexibility. Whether you're scaling globally from day one or expanding one market at a time, success depends on understanding your approach, building a strong foundation, and tailoring your strategy for each new market. By following a structured execution plan, you can minimize risks, gain traction, and position your business for long-term success.

* * *

Key Takeaways

- **Theory vs. Practice**: This book equips founders and service providers with proven methods to boost revenue, but real-world application often reveals unforeseen challenges. Navigating the gap between theory and practice is an essential part of the sales journey.

- **Managing Typical Situations**: Founders face numerous practical steps in their sales and marketing journeys, from LinkedIn outreach and prospect qualification to content creation and international expansion. Applying these frameworks enables them to address challenges in sales, marketing, and operational growth effectively.

- **Learning Through Practice**: Success rarely comes on the first try, and mastering any skill requires time, effort, and persistence. Fine tune approaches to suit your style, stay consistent in execution, and remember that challenges are a natural part of the journey— progress comes with practice.

CHAPTER 7

Putting *The Launch Code* to Work

"Vision without execution is hallucination."
– Thomas Edison

The year was 1999, and Los Angeles was buzzing with the energy of the dotcom era. I spent my days sitting in my glass-walled office at CBS, where I held a coveted position as vice president in the company's corporate sales and marketing division. Outside my window, the city glimmered with opportunity, but inside, I felt restless. Everywhere, people my age were leaving their corporate jobs to chase the promise of the internet. Companies like Amazon and eBay were just a few years old, and the digital frontier felt wide open. The idea of staying in the comfort of a traditional career, watching others take risks, became unbearable.

So, I made the leap from vision to execution. My wife and I packed up our lives and moved to Budapest, where, together with my brother, we launched what we envisioned would become the "Yahoo of Central and Eastern Europe." Our plan was ambitious: build a network of local news and information portals for the region's emerging internet users. We raised $1.5 million from thirty angel investors and started building eEuropeMedia.

The early days were exhilarating. I traded in corporate structure and a steady paycheck for the chaos and freedom of startup life, which was both liberating and terrifying. There's a unique thrill in creating something out of nothing—in convincing investors, employees, and customers to believe in our vision. But the highs came with devastating lows. The relentless grind of managing cash flow, navigating personal and professional conflicts, and facing unforeseen obstacles daily, tested me in ways I never expected. Every step forward felt hard-won; every setback felt monumental.

Yet, amid the struggle, there were moments of triumph. One of the most unforgettable was the day I convinced Hewlett-Packard to partner with us. At the time, digital photography was in its infancy, and the company believed it could lead this emerging market. Our portal resonated with tech-savvy young users and so it seemed like we could support their strategy by creating a dedicated web channel. Still, the idea of pitching HP, a global tech giant, with our scrappy startup, felt audacious.

I'll never forget walking into HP's offices, armed with little more than a PowerPoint presentation and sheer conviction. We didn't have a polished product or a big name behind us. What we had was a deep understanding of their needs and an unshakeable belief in our solution. I poured my heart into that pitch, showing them not just what we had built, but the potential it held to reshape the industry. Against all odds, they said yes.

That moment taught me a powerful lesson: founder-led sales is about focused execution. It's about deeply understanding a customer's problem and offering a solution with passion and persistence. If you can master these qualities, you can sell anything.

It's Time to Take Action

You now have at your disposal a comprehensive toolkit of strategies and tactics to accelerate your revenue growth. But beyond the methodology, I hope you've embraced a new mindset. You've moved past the misconception

> *"Founder-led sales is about focused execution. It's about deeply understanding a customer's problem and offering a solution with passion and persistence."*

that sales is manipulative and you see it for what it truly is—it's about solving problems, providing value, and demonstrating your unique approach. This shift is crucial not just for closing deals but for building a business with genuine impact.

Now comes the hard part: putting what you've learned into action. The good news? Many founders before you have applied *The Launch Code* successfully. Listen to what they've achieved and, more importantly, how applying this blueprint to their business transformed their businesses and lives.

- **Marton Demeter, Founder and CEO of HMMConsultant**: "The biggest gain I walked away with was a change in mindset. Since last October–November, we've been closing more and more big deals. It feels like a chain reaction started, and bigger projects keep coming our way."

- **Radek Novotny, Co-Founder and CEO of Superface.ai**:

  "For technical people like me, sales is a black box. I feel much safer now that I have a solution for these challenges. I have this framework and materials that show me specific steps. I'm more confident about what to do. I learned how to think about sales in a different way."

- **Steve Ruszina, CEO and Co-Founder of Invention Factory**:

  "I now have a clear thought process to make sure I understand what I'm selling and who I'm selling it to. If I follow the process, it's easier to look at things from my customer's perspective. The biggest benefit for me is that I have a completely different mindset about sales."

- **Simon Neal, Founder and CEO of CampMap**:

  "*The Launch Code* was a game changer for me as a technical founder with no sales or marketing experience. I really needed concrete information and processes to get our growth engine working. *The Launch Code* provides everything you need as a founder to execute successfully. Now I know how to market and sell our product."

The common thread? These founders embraced new strategies, honed essential skills, and transformed their mindset from fear and doubt to clarity and confidence. That's the exact journey I hope to inspire for you.

Now, I understand that making such a significant shift isn't easy. That's why I'd like to share two powerful exercises—creating a *Destination Plan* and a *Blast Off! Blueprint*—that will help you take that first step and guide you on your journey.

Set Your Business's Destination

Destination planning is like dreaming with a deadline.

Most of us start a business driven by a vision—a future we're determined to create. But amid the whirlwind of daily tasks and competing priorities, it's easy to lose sight of that dream. That's why it's crucial to pause and reflect on your purpose: *why* you're doing *what* you do and what success genuinely looks like for you.

Your *Destination Plan* will serve as your North Star. Like the guiding light sailors once relied on to navigate vast and unpredictable seas, your Destination provides a steady point of focus. No matter how turbulent the waters become, it will keep you aligned with your goals and moving in the right direction. This

> *"It's crucial to pause and reflect on your purpose: why you're doing what you do and what success genuinely looks like for you."*

simple yet powerful tool ensures that your daily actions stay connected to your larger vision, fueling your inspiration along the way.

A *Destination Plan* is built on two essential components:

1. **Your Greater Purpose**: The deeper motivation for building your business, extending beyond fame and fortune to the meaningful value you aim to create in the world.

2. **Your Desired Outcome**: A vivid, detailed snapshot of what your business will look like at a specific point in the future. This vision brings your goals to life and makes them tangible.

Follow these steps to create your *Destination Plan*:

Step 1: Define Your Greater Purpose: Ask yourself: "Why am I building this business?" "How will it create meaningful change and deliver value to others?" Condense your answer into a few sentences.

Emi Gal founded the healthcare AI startup Ezra with a deeply personal purpose: to revolutionize early cancer detection through full-body MRI screening, focusing on high-risk individuals like himself. Emi advises founders to "start with a clear sense of mission—something that deeply motivates you on a personal level."

Step 2: Envision Your Desired Outcome: Imagine your business eighteen to twenty-four months from now—a time that's far enough away to allow for meaningful progress but close enough to feel achievable. Describe its key aspects in the *present tense* (i.e., "there are," not "there will be"), covering areas such as:

- **Product**: How has it evolved? What improvements have you made? What feedback are you receiving?

- **Sales and Marketing**: How many clients do you have? What's your revenue? How effective is your lead generation?

- **Team and Organization**: Are you still a small, tight-knit group, or have you scaled to a larger organization with global reach?

- **Finances**: What's your cash flow? Have you attracted investment, or are you self-sustaining?

- **Other Key Aspects**: Think about anything else that defines your success—whether it's awards, recognition, or impact.

Your Desired Outcome should be realistic, but bold. If it doesn't scare you a little, it's probably not ambitious enough.

Step 3: Feel Your Destination: Visualize how you'll feel when you've achieved your Destination. Will you feel proud of your achievements? Energized by new opportunities? Fulfilled by the feedback from customers? Create a strong emotional connection to this outcome to become even more motivated.

Put Your Destination to Work

Now that you've created your *Destination Plan*, here's how to use it to stay focused and aligned with your vision:

Keep It Top of Mind: Develop a shorthand for your Destination—whether it's a few key words, a symbol, or an image—that encapsulates the core of your vision and the emotions tied to achieving it. Display this reminder somewhere you'll see daily, like your bathroom mirror, phone wallpaper, or computer screen. A simple, consistent cue can serve as a powerful motivator.

Share and Align Your Destination: Your Destination isn't just for you; it's a guiding light for everyone involved in your business. Share it with your co-founders, team members, and investors to ensure alignment. Better yet, involve your team in creating the Destination to incorporate diverse perspectives, build shared ownership, and craft an outcome that resonates with everyone.

Work Backward to Plan Forward: Treat your Destination as the endpoint in your goal-setting process (outlined in Chapter 5). Break down the journey into actionable steps, starting with the Desired Outcome and working backward. This approach keeps your actions purposeful and your path clear, leading directly toward your ultimate goals.

9-3-1 'Blast Off!'

Your second execution aid is the *Blast Off! Blueprint*—a tool that helps you decide which of *The Launch Code's* strategies and tactics are most likely to accelerate your revenue growth. This exercise helps you sift through the

> *"This exercise helps you sift through the dozens of potential actions and identify your top priorities."*

dozens of potential actions and identify your top priorities.

Here's how to use it:

Step 1: Identify One Action Per Module: Review each of *The Launch Code's* nine modules and pick one action per module that you will implement to boost the effectiveness of your sales and marketing. For example:

- *Module 1: Value Proposition*

  Organize a meeting with my marketing manager to update our current value proposition using the five-step framework.

- *Module 5: Partnerships*

  Define ten target distributors and aggregators for the UK market and identify a touchpoint for each.

- *Module 8: Performance Tracking*

  Create a management dashboard to track your top three operational KPIs.

Step 2: Prioritize Top 3 Actions: Out of the nine actions, choose the top three that will have the greatest impact on your business. Commit to executing them over the next four to six weeks. As you complete each action, replace it with another from your list, ensuring that you are always focused on the highest priorities.

Step 3: Choose Today's Action: Pick one of your Top 3 actions and take immediate steps to get it started. This could be as simple as sending an email, researching a website, or making a phone call. The key is to *do it*.

Your *Blast Off! Blueprint* is a powerful tool to help you implement *The Launch Code* in your business. Don't be fooled by its simplicity—there's nothing more effective than narrowing your focus and taking that first action. It sets everything else in motion, propelling your business toward success.

Harness the Power of Persistence

Building a business is one of the most challenging and rewarding journeys you can undertake. It's your chance to shape the future, live by your values, and create something meaningful. But let's be real—it's tough. You'll face obstacles you never anticipated, even with this book as your guide. Convincing others to believe in your vision will test your patience and resolve, especially in a world where criticism is plentiful. But, believe me, it's worth it.

Take the story of my friend and classmate, Marc Wallace, a serial entrepreneur, as a testament to the power of persistence. After starting his career as an aerospace engineer, Marc launched SwapDrive, an early precursor to today's cloud storage platforms. While many in our group of college friends followed traditional career paths in finance, media, and industry, Marc took on the grueling challenge of building a tech startup.

We stayed in touch over the years, catching up at the usual events that bring old friends together—bachelor parties, weddings, and college reunions. While most of us shared updates about promotions and career milestones, Marc kept quiet about the less glamorous side of building his business. We knew he was working on something big, but few of us fully understood what he was up to.

Then, in 2009, Marc sold his company to Symantec for over $100 million.

A decade later, I spoke with Marc about his journey building SwapDrive. He shared that it was far tougher than he ever anticipated. He recalled at least four occasions when he came home and told his wife, "We're done. We don't have enough money to make payroll." Some of his fellow entrepreneurs, facing the same challenges, shut down their businesses. Marc, however, explained, "The difference between me and those other guys was persistence: I just stuck with it and figured it out."

Since then, Marc has co-founded two other successful ventures: Radius Networks (Flybuy.com), an AI platform that uses mobile location to optimize staff operations and the guest experience for brands across more than 50 countries and 30,000 locations, and District Taco, a Yucatan-style Mexican restaurant chain with 18 locations and growing.

Building a business is an emotional rollercoaster. Some days, you'll feel like you're on top of the world; others, you'll feel like you're plummeting downward without brakes. But the satisfaction of creating something meaningful is unparalleled. It's the grind and pushing through the tough times that leads to success.

So, as you apply the mindset, strategies, and tactics in this book to your business, remember that persistence will be your greatest ally. If you encounter setbacks, don't get discouraged—just keep moving forward, one step at a time.

It's fitting that I close this book with a quote from Calvin Coolidge, the thirtieth President of the United States. I memorized his words at age nineteen and have leaned on them throughout my life and career ever since. I hope they will inspire and guide you on your path to boosting your revenue growth and becoming a successful founder.

"Nothing in the world can take the place of persistence. Talent will not; nothing is more common than unsuccessful men with talent. Genius will not; unrewarded genius is almost a proverb. Education will not; the world is full of educated derelicts. Persistence and determination alone are all-powerful. The slogan 'press on' has solved and will always solve the problems of the human race."

Now, press on. Your journey is just beginning.

* * *

Key Takeaways

- **Take Action to Transform Your Business**: Success comes from taking action. By shifting your mindset from self-doubt to confidence, embracing new sales strategies and honing your skills, you'll elevate your business and yourself.

- **Define Your Vision and Prioritize Efforts**: A clear *Destination Plan* and a *Blast Off! Blueprint* will help you align daily actions with your larger goals. Create a bold yet realistic vision and identify high-priority tasks, so you take your first steps toward accelerating growth.

- **Persistence is Your Greatest Ally**: Building a business is challenging, and setbacks are inevitable. Success requires patience, resilience, and consistent effort. Stay the course, refine your strategies, and move forward—progress comes one step at a time.

Please Review My Book

If you enjoyed my book, please leave a review on Amazon or Goodreads. I read every review, and it will help more founders discover and benefit from *The Launch Code*.

Use this QR code to review on **Amazon**.

Use this QR code to review on **Goodreads**.

How I Can Help

If you need additional support to implement *The Launch Code* in your business, choose from these options:

- **Buy** *The Launch Code* **video course** for access to explanations, worksheets, and tools you can apply at your own pace.

- **Join** *The Launch Code* **group program** for a collaborative learning experience with other founders.

- **Sign up for personal mentoring** to receive tailored implementation support or advisory services.

- **Organize a live workshop** for your team or company.

- **Book me to speak** at an event or conference.

For details, visit www.zoltanvardy.com or contact me at zoltan.vardy@thelaunchcode.net.

Use this QR code to access my latest offers!

Acknowledgments

Writing a book has been on my bucket list since I was a teenager. It took me a while, but here we are. I can finally cross it off. This book is the product of a fifty-four-year journey, shaped by countless people. While I can't name everyone, I'd like to shine a light on a few who made especially meaningful contributions along the way.

First, to my parents, Drs. Steven and Agnes Vardy: prolific authors and academic powerhouses who set the bar incredibly high and somehow made me believe I could clear it. Thank you for challenging and encouraging me, Nicholas, and Laura, and for showing us that big ideas belong in books. To my wife, Lili: for over thirty years, you've been my partner through every high, low, and international move. Your patience is otherworldly, and your love and support are my foundation. And to Szofi, our incredible daughter: you turned my focus from career to family in the most beautiful way. You remind me every day that "Apa" is the best title I'll ever hold.

Then there are the professional influences who shaped me. Bosses like Tom Bates, Dan Lovinger, Bill Apfelbaum, David Stogel, Patrick Tillieux, and Satpal Brainch—you offered me mentorship, friendship, served as role models, and opened doors to professional opportunities that changed the trajectory of my career. To my colleagues at TV2: working with you was nothing short of extraordinary. We scaled mountains together, and I've never been part of a more inspiring, driven, and accomplished team.

Fast forward to today, when my work wouldn't exist without the support of a few key people. Enikő Domján, you've been there from

Day One of *The Launch Code*—shaping my ideas, managing my personal brand, and ensuring the important stuff got done. Thanks go to you and Andrea Stolczenberger, my doppelgänger on social media, and Dávid Eszenyi, the wizard who makes the tech work.

A word of thanks to my clients—every individual and company I've sold to over the past thirty years. Our work together shaped the core principles of this book. A special thanks to the over 200 startup founders who have embraced *The Launch Code*, inspiring me with your passion and helping refine the framework to solve your biggest challenges.

Finally, a shout out goes to the silent forces behind this book: Rob Wolf Petersen, for guiding its structure and sharpening my ideas; Tom Bates, Julian Coustaury, and Attila Gazdag, for your honest and invaluable feedback—it made all the difference.

Writing a book is not for the faint-hearted. It's been exhausting, humbling, and, at times, downright maddening. But I'm incredibly proud of the end result. It was hard as hell—but hey, so is anything worth doing.

Cheers to the journey!